SET APART

DISCOVERING
Personal VICTORY
THROUGH *Holiness*

SET APART

DISCOVERING *Personal* VICTORY THROUGH *Holiness*

BRUCE WILKINSON

Multnomah® Publishers *Sisters, Oregon*

SET APART
published by Multnomah Publishers, Inc.
© 1998, 2003 by Bruce Wilkinson
International Standard Book Number: 1-59052-071-8

Revised edition. Previously published in 1998 as
Personal Holiness in Times of Temptation by Harvest House Publishers.

Cover image by Steve Gardner

Unless otherwise noted, Scripture quotations in this book are taken from
The Holy Bible, New King James Version © 1984 by Thomas Nelson, Inc.
Other Scripture quotations from:
New American Standard Bible (NASB) © 1960, 1977
by the Lockman Foundation
Young's Literal Translation of the Holy Bible (YLT), Robert Young, 1898.
The Holy Bible, New International Version (NIV)
© 1973, 1984 by International Bible Society,
used by permission of Zondervan Publishing House
It is the author's intent to emphasize certain portions of Scripture by italicizing them.
These changes are solely the author's and do not reflect the original text.

Multnomah is a trademark of Multnomah Publishers, Inc.,
and is registered in the U.S. Patent and Trademark Office.
The colophon is a trademark of Multnomah Publishers, Inc.

For information:
MULTNOMAH PUBLISHERS, INC. • P.O. BOX 1720 • SISTERS, OR 97759

Library of Congress Cataloging-in-Publication Data

Wilkinson, Bruce.
    Set apart / by Bruce Wilkinson.
        p. cm.
    Rev. ed. of: Personal holiness in time of temptation. c1998.
    ISBN 1-59052-071-8
    1. Holiness. 2. Temptation. 3. Spiritual life—Christianity. I. Wilkinson, Bruce.
Personal holiness in time of temptation. II. Title.

    BT767 .W55 2003
    234'.8—dc21

                                        2002152491

03 04 05 06 07 08 09—10 9 8 7 6 5 4 3 2 1 0

Table of Contents

Introduction

What? Me, Holy?

*When we think of holiness, great saints of the past like Francis of
Assisi or George Mueller spring to mind—or contemporary
giants of the faith like Mother Teresa. But holiness is not the private preserve
of an elite corps of martyrs, mystics, and Nobel Prize winners.
Holiness is the everyday business of every Christian.*

CHUCK COLSON

*P*icture yourself interviewing for the ideal job. Each part of
the interview process has gone well, and today is the
final test: a meeting with the president. After the normal
small talk, he asks an unexpected question: "If you were to describe
yourself with just five words, what would they be?"

Your heart pounds as you search for the best answer—how can
someone summarize him- or herself in only five words? As your
mind races, you notice the president reach across his desk to a small
stack of index cards with lists of words on them. Sensing your dis-
comfort, he slowly shuffles through the cards and says, "Don't be so
tough on yourself. Just pick five words. Our personnel department
already spoke to a number of your friends, family members, and a

few of your previous work associates and asked the same question. We're just curious to see if your responses line up with how everyone else sees you."

You reflect on that for a moment. What words would *others* use to describe you? If the president slid those cards across the desk for you to read, what words would you find on them?

Would any of those people have put the word *godly* on the list?

Would you select the word *holy* to describe your life?

If you're like most people, the thought of calling yourself holy probably never entered your mind. The concept of being holy seems to be one of those qualities reserved for Sunday mornings or to describe saints and missionaries, not people like you and me.

One Saturday morning, I tried this experiment with a couple dozen men from my home church. After asking them to write down the five words that best described themselves, I asked if any had written the word *holy*. The answer was an embarrassed silence. A few rocked back in their chairs, some folded their arms, and most looked around the room, trying not to make eye contact.

When I asked why they felt uncomfortable describing themselves as holy, the men had no problem relating their reasons: "Being holy is for preachers! I'd use it to describe a martyr or a missionary, but not me! It's for saints, not sinners. Maybe when I'm dead I can be holy, but right now I'm just a normal guy." In the minds of most "normal guys," holiness exists out there somewhere with dusty, distant, or dead saints—not riding around in trucks, wearing boots, and working nine to five.

Wanting to better understand their attitudes toward holiness, I asked the men to describe a holy person. They offered examples like these:

"Holiness means stern people wearing dark colors and high black stockings, walking in rigid strides."

"People who would write *holy* on their sheets live hard lives with hidden troubles, carrying big black Bibles around to remind them of what they shouldn't be doing."

"To be holy is to live in the Valley of No—say no to everything that has color, joy, spontaneity, humor, variety, creativity. Like football, music with a beat, and a thick, medium-rare T-bone steak!"

Then one guy, the wit of the group, gave this answer: "Holiness is like that famous painting of the old couple, the one where they're standing sternly next to their barn and the husband's holding a pitchfork."

At that, everyone exploded with laughter. In their minds, he nailed it. We define holiness with words like *sober, sad, boring, tight,* and *superreligious;* but we rarely define it as something real or recent.

The more I listened that morning, the easier it was to understand why no one put *holy* on his list. Who wants to stand around stiffly in a starched shirt, pitchfork in hand?

The deeper I probed, the more depressed I became. I knew these men weren't alone. In fact, theirs is a common reaction to being called *holy.* Holiness is a welcome discard from a previous generation. People seem almost relieved that holiness lies buried in the dim past, and most don't want to return and dig up its tattered, undesired remains.

A Holy Mess

Scattered over the top of my worktable were pages of verses on the subject of holiness taken from throughout the Word of God. After serious consideration, I had decided to address this vitally important subject in a book that would change how people think about being holy. But first I determined to set aside everything I believed about holiness and start all over—with just the Bible and a fresh slate—to make sure that I let the Bible speak for itself instead of my speaking for it.

The pages before me listed all the Bible verses translated from the root word for *holy* regardless of how they were translated into the English language. As I read these verses, words such as *holy, holiness, sanctify, set apart,* and *separated* threaded their way through the pages. For some reason, I had expected this to be a relatively easy step in the developmental process, but my expectations were far from reality. Little did I anticipate that this task initially would create for me more frustration and confusion than insight and clarity.

The problem surfaced almost immediately: How could this root concept of holiness be revealed in the Bible as something that had already happened, in other verses as something that should happen in the present, then in still other verses as something that will happen later? How could holiness be in some verses something Jesus did for me totally, in other verses something the Holy Spirit does in me, and in still other verses a commandment for me to be holy and live in a holy manner?

The more I read, the more confused I became! Was I already holy or not? If I *was* holy, then why did the Bible command me to *live* holy? How could believers who were called holy in one verse, later *in the same chapter* be strongly exhorted to stop living such sinful lives? How could they be holy if they were unholy?

Time after time I felt waves of frustration. Instead of unraveling holiness and presenting it in a clear and helpful format, I found myself struggling with a tangled mess of fishing line. I could take a handful of these verses and prove to you that you are already holy, so live what you are. I could take another handful of verses and prove that you will be holy one day, so you had better keep working on it.

No wonder there are so many different viewpoints on this intriguing and intricate subject. At this point, I entertained serious thoughts about letting someone else write this book! Why write a book about a subject on which so many godly people disagree? Why risk offending someone?

If the men and women who were present when I first taught this material hadn't responded so profoundly to what the Lord did in their hearts as a result, I would have abandoned the project on the worktable.

But through the difficult process of clarification, I became convinced that this shouldn't be a book on the theology of holiness. In fact, you won't find even a single footnote in these pages. I won't be evaluating anyone else's viewpoint on the subject. Nor will I examine all the fine points of any Scripture passage.

Why not? Because I have a different goal in mind.

REPOSITIONING HOLINESS

Positioning is a marketing concept that was birthed and came of age in the late twentieth century. This concept tells us that a product or service is "positioned" in the mind of the public to evoke a certain emotional response. Positioning can happen by way of a well-orchestrated, highly financed media campaign. Or it may happen in response to cultural events beyond the control of any advertising agency or public relations firm. But when a product is purposely "repositioned," people are expected to respond to the product in a dramatically different manner.

In post–World War II America, the words *Made in Japan* on a product failed to evoke a positive emotional response in the consumer. But today, in a world economy driven by demand for high technology, Japanese exports have become highly desirable in the United States and around the world. Not many of us wanted to purchase a Datsun before 1980, but today the names Toyota, Nissan, Honda, Lexus, and Infiniti dominate automobile sales. As Japan's positioning in the American and world marketplace changed, so did consumers' purchasing habits.

We need to reposition holiness in the hearts and minds of the church.

The enemy has orchestrated a long, relentless, strategic campaign to position holiness as something to be avoided at all costs.

The picture most of us have concerning holiness is simply not true. The holy among us are not just stern people wearing dark colors. Those who see themselves as holy don't necessarily live in the Valley of No. Indeed, a life spent in pursuit of holiness is a wild, daring, robust life that most would envy if they understood the truth.

C. S. Lewis once wrote, "How little people know who think that holiness is dull. When one meets the real thing, it is irresistible! If even 10 percent of the world's population had it, would not the whole world be converted and happy before a year's end?" Do you suppose Lewis is correct? Could it be that when you meet a person who is genuinely holy, he or she is one of the few who are genuinely happy?

Holiness has been positioned in most minds as something undesirable, even harmful—and many have paid dearly for their mistake. I want to share with you what the Bible *really* says about holiness, and I unabashedly seek to reposition holiness in your mind and in your life as you read this book.

PART ONE

Turning Your Heart Toward Holiness

Chapter 1

Personal Holiness

The destined end of man is not happiness, nor health, but holiness.
God is not an eternal blessing machine for men.
He did not come to save men out of pity;
He came to save men because He had created them to be holy.

OSWALD CHAMBERS

*T*he theology professor walked into the lecture hall for the final class of his fifty-year teaching career. The auditorium buzzed with the usual before-class chatter. The professor was about to complete his teaching, entitled "The Life of Holiness." Holiness was a favorite topic of his, but throughout the semester a bitter undercurrent of argument and debate had marred the graduate-level class. No one, it seemed, could agree on the meaning of holiness. One group of students claimed that holiness had to be lived one way, while another faction claimed that a life of holiness was not even possible. All had a Scripture verse to back up their individual claims, and nobody would back down or even listen to another's reasoning or perspective.

Now the professor looked out over the lecture hall. Pockets of students sat in isolated clusters. The conflicting theological divisions in the auditorium had dogmatically and harshly argued with each other, to the point that they had physically and emotionally separated from one another. For nearly the entire semester, he had labored to break through their judgmental attitudes and independent spirits. After pacing for days in his book-lined basement library, searching for a possible solution, he had come up with one last idea.

The professor slowly wrote one solitary word on the middle of the blackboard. He then stared at it, drawing every eye in the classroom to the one word: *trunks.*

He turned to face the class and in measured tones said, "This session may be the most challenging of your graduate career. Please discuss and define this word with the students seated around you and list every reason why you believe your definition is correct. Do not discuss your thoughts with another group. No questions will be entertained at the lectern. In ten minutes, be prepared for your group's official spokesperson to stand and read your written answer."

A long pause followed. The professor then said, "Let me advise you from the outset, students, that there is only one correct answer to this question, and your written answer will weigh heavily on your final grade for this class." With that sobering revelation, he calmly turned on his heel and walked resolutely from the room. The corners of his mouth twitched upward ever so slightly as he walked down the hallway, wondering about the debates raging back in his classroom.

Ten minutes passed. He strode back into the room, opened his grade book, faced the class, and asked for a group to volunteer. No one spoke. The professor waited for what seemed an eternity. "Then, if no one will volunteer, this option is hereby closed. Please pass forward your written statements with the name of each person in your group signed at the bottom."

From the back of the room came a rumbling. "This isn't fair! What do trunks have to do with a life of holiness?" Without acknowledging the outburst, the professor turned to the blackboard and in front of the word *trunks* added three more words: *the big gray.*

"After further consideration," he said, "I've softened my previous position and decided to give you a second chance. Follow the same instructions precisely. Let me advise you again, there is only *one correct answer* and your written answer will weigh heavily on your final grade." The classroom nearly exploded in frustration. But the professor quietly departed.

Ten long minutes passed before he returned to the same stupefied silence. Once again, the groups' papers were collected and neatly stacked on top of the previous ones, deliberately placed next to his grade book.

For a third time, the professor turned toward the board. This time he added six words. The board now read, *The big gray trunks bounced down the dusty African road.* With exaggerated emphasis, he placed the period at the end of the sentence.

"After further deliberation, I have elected to provide you a third opportunity. Follow the same instructions precisely. Let me advise you again, there is only *one correct answer* and your written answer will weigh heavily on your final grade." He paused for a minute before adding, "Oh, and because of the importance of this paper on your theological future, after you have completed your answer, please debate your findings with the groups around you in order to consider all perspectives."

As the professor left the room this time, he turned to the right and headed upstairs to the sound booth overlooking the auditorium. He wanted to observe firsthand the results of his assignment.

Chaos reigned below as the students vented their pent-up frustrations. Debates and arguments flooded the room, not only between groups but also within groups. Voices were raised and arms waved. Finally, after fifteen minutes of discussion, the professor decided to cut off the debate.

For the final time, he entered the auditorium and began to challenge the students' thinking. First, he asked the various groups to list on the board what the word *trunks* meant in the context of the sentence. There were four different interpretations: the trunk of a car, the trunk of an elephant, a suitcase or chest, and the midsection of a person's body.

The professor then asked whether anyone had changed his or her mind in the course of the debate. Almost all admitted that they had changed their answer at least once. The professor repeated his assertion that there was only one correct answer and then asked the groups if any would like to risk their semester's grade on their response. No one moved. "Why won't you risk your grade?" he questioned. "Aren't you *sure* you know the answer?"

A student in the back nearly yelled, "No, because we don't have all the necessary information!" For once, heads all around nodded in agreement.

Slowly the professor nodded and turned yet again to the board. With great care, he touched his chalk to the period at the end of the sentence and dramatically added a long tail, making it a comma. He scanned the faces in the room, heightening the implications of his unexpected action. Then he finished the sentence: *The big gray trunks bounced down the dusty African road, as the boy who was wearing them ran by.*

Everyone groaned. Not one group had come up with the correct answer. With the first smile of the day, the professor asked a pivotal question: "Now how many of you would be willing to take another shot at it and risk your semester's grade on your answer?" Every hand shot up. "What changed to make your confidence so complete?"

One of the older members of the class, a young man who spoke only on rare occasions, stood and summarized for everyone. "We finally have all the parts we need for the answer. Before we had only one word, and we were wrong. Then we knew only fragments, and still we were wrong. Then when you wrote about 'bouncing down an African road,' most of us changed our minds, thinking we finally had the answer. It was only after you gave us the complete sentence that we knew the whole truth."

The professor nodded. "So what percentage of you were mistaken about your earlier answers?"

"One hundred percent."

"That's right—all of you were mistaken. Despite the intense debates, all of you were wrong! Even though some of you were sure of your position, you did not have adequate information to believe so. We can't be dogmatic about things unless we have all the information."

Then, turning back to the board, he added, "Now let me ask you what another word means." With that the professor erased the sentence on the board and wrote the word *holiness*. Understanding flooded the classroom.

At that moment, the bell rang. The professor laid down his chalk and said, "Make sure you have all the information before making your decision." Then he smiled gently and walked to the door. Thundering applause erupted from the students, whose hearts had been touched by the truth.

Now that you are pursuing holiness, do you know where you're going and what you're looking for? Will you know when you have hit the target—not in your eyes, but in heaven's eyes? After all, holiness is not a human thought; it's a supernatural thought, right from the very throne of heaven.

If you are a bit unsure, then perhaps you may decide to stick around for a few moments after class.

HOLINESS MEANS SEPARATION

The first step in pursuing holiness starts with a clear understanding of what God means by holiness. Holiness has been defined by individuals and denominations in all kinds of ways—with as much resulting rancor and emotional baggage as experienced in that classroom. The root concept of holiness is unmistakable, however, and is exposed in the Bible through the drama of the burning bush:

> Then Moses said, "I will now turn aside and see this great sight, why the bush does not burn." So when the LORD saw that he turned aside to look, God called to him from the midst of the bush and said, "Moses, Moses!" And he said, "Here I am." Then He said, "Do not draw near this place. Take your sandals off your feet, for the place where you stand is *holy ground.*" (Exodus 3:3–5)

Holy ground? How could ground be holy? If Moses had taken a handful of "unholy" ground and compared it with the "holy" sand at the burning bush, would he have seen the difference? If during the previous week Moses had shepherded his flock through that same patch of the desert, would it have been holy then? Or if Moses had taken a few grains of holy sand back to his tent and studied them carefully, would he have discovered that the nature of the sand had been changed or that it was still just plain old desert dirt? Why did the Lord declare this ground to be holy?

Holiness Means Separation

If you had a big Hebrew dictionary sitting within arm's reach like I do, you could soon find the answer. You would quickly discover that the root concept of holiness lies in the word *separation*. The ground became holy simply because God separated it as the unique place where He would reveal Himself to Moses. In a sense, all the rest of the desert remained unholy because God didn't choose it to be the location for this meeting. If God had moved a stone's throw to the north and spoken there, that particular part of the desert would have been called holy.

Imagine that after one of the massive feasts conducted during King Solomon's reign, one of the temple priests went home to his wife with a request. "Sweetheart, I need a new holy knife for the temple. All of the knives there have dulled, so would you mind if I took one of ours?" The instant the priest dedicated the knife to the Lord's service, that unholy kitchen knife became a holy temple knife.

Holiness can describe the "separation" in a person's mind regarding a knife, a plot of ground, a city, or many other things. I call this mental holiness, as the separation occurs only in the person's thinking. For example, not only did the fundamental nature of the sand not change, but no one would have known the ground was "holy" unless God revealed it to him.

Holiness Requires Both Separation From and Separation To

Holiness requires *separation from* one thing and *separation to* a different thing. Think about that for a moment, and it becomes obvious that you can't have one without the other. For that knife to become holy it must be *separated from* the house and *separated to* the temple.

Throughout the Old and New Testaments, the root word *holy* and its derivatives are translated into such terms as *set apart, dedicated, consecrated, sanctified, holy, separated,* and *saint.* Whatever their particular context in the Bible, each is rooted in the concept of separateness. Holiness requires division. Up to the moment the temple priest took the knife *from* his home, that knife couldn't become holy. Why not? Because it was with all the other knives and not distinct. Until the Lord set that particular part of the desert apart from the rest of the desert, He couldn't call it holy. Holiness, then, requires withdrawal. Holiness requires disconnection. For a person to become holy in this sense, he must depart from anything unholy, or holiness is impossible.

The second side of separation requires that the knife become *united or devoted to* something else. The priest took the knife from the kitchen and placed it in the temple. Holiness requires reconnection.

Holiness requires subtraction *and* addition. New people, new practices, and new pursuits must be added to your life to replace the old unholy patterns. We *abandon* our unholy ways and *pursue* His holy way. Without both aspects of this separation, biblical holiness is simply not possible.

The believer must flee from something and then follow after something else. We find these two distinct parts in 2 Timothy 2:22:

> *Flee* [separate yourself from] also youthful lusts; but *pursue* [separate yourself to] righteousness, faith, love, peace with those who call on the Lord out of a pure heart.

So much of the negative perception regarding holiness is a result of harsh teaching and fiery sermons on "fleeing." Holiness is not about living in the world of No; it's about leaving the world of No in order to enter the world of Yes! But whenever a person seeks to fulfill only one half of this equation—pursuing righteousness without fleeing youthful lusts, for example—imbalance and error will eventually disrupt his life.

But practical holiness for the Christian occurs when we leave behind the patterns of this world in order to become more Christlike in our character and conduct. The apostle Peter wrote:

> But as He who called you is holy, you also be holy in all your conduct, because it is written, "Be holy, for I am holy." (1 Peter 1:15–16)

This is a person-to-person call placed by the Lord God to you. The Lord is calling you to be holy. He beckons you to come out from all conduct that is inappropriate and be separated to Him, to depart from everything that isn't like Him and devote yourself fully to Him.

You see, holiness is the center of God's will for you. The Holy One Himself wants you to be holy. May your heart discover the incredible power of release and reattachment. May you depart from all that isn't holy and pursue all that is.

Holiness Has Standards

Every known culture in this world honors some form of holiness. Certain places and practices are described as "sacred," while others are called "taboo." Both of these terms describe the issue of separation from that which is secular to that which is sacred.

When a husband and wife experience trauma in their lives and choose to separate from one another and live independent lives, no one would call them holy, would they? Why not?

Holiness Requires Separation from the Secular to the Sacred

Holy separation requires separation from that which is secular to that which is sacred. Pagan cultures have "holy men" who have separated and devoted themselves to the pursuit of their tribal deities and their supposed powers over nature, sickness, crops, and enemies. But the Bible tells us that all believers are called to leave unholiness behind and pursue the truth of God. Whatever you choose to separate yourself *from,* you must choose to separate yourself *to* the Lord.

We read in Scripture of the holy temple, the holy Sabbath, a holy altar, and holy places. These places and things were separated from the natural and devoted to the supernatural, from the service of man to the service of God. Occasionally, I am asked to publicly dedicate a room or building to the Lord. In a true sense, that room or building becomes sanctified, or set apart to the Lord, His work, and His glory. The building becomes holy unto the Lord.

Darlene Marie and I have devoted our home and all our belongings to the Lord. First we walked around the plot of ground we purchased and dedicated it to the Lord and His glory. Then we stood together and specifically dedicated our home and everything in it to the Lord and His service. The house remained a regular home in the eyes of our neighbors and passersby; but when we devoted it to Him, the property transitioned into the realm of holiness. Now we are but stewards of His assets and workers in His home.

You see, separation occurs not only in the tangible but also in the intangible, in the seen and the unseen. Likewise, a person can choose to devote his heart, soul, and might to the Lord, thereby separating himself to the Lord in his own heart and mind. Perhaps you've attended the ordination of a minister to the Lord. At the most solemn moment in the service, the individual will be asked to kneel before the congregation and the elders will lay their hands on him and officially dedicate and devote him to the Lord and His service. You would be correct in thinking this is a holy ceremony in a holy place for a holy purpose, resulting in the official devotion of a holy person.

Holiness is God's will for your life.

When the nation of Israel agreed to be God's holy nation, the Lord outlined some rather unusual ways in which He wanted them to separate themselves from all other nations. The Lord said to them, "You shall be holy, for I the LORD your God am holy" (Leviticus 19:1). He then gave them a series of specific "holiness regulations" to constantly remind the Jews and everyone around them that they weren't just any nation; they belonged to the Lord, a fact which influenced everything in their lives. Consider two of these laws:

> "You shall not sow your field with mixed seed. Nor shall a garment of mixed linen and wool come upon you." (Leviticus 19:19)

In other words, for a Jew to be ceremonially holy, he could not sow two different kinds of seeds in his garden or wear a blended shirt. He would have to wear an all-wool shirt. These specific and unique laws were given to the Jews to distinguish and separate them from everyone else. Every morning as they dressed they were reminded that because they were the Lord's nation, they were separate from other nations and were called to practice separation. Of course, the wearing of an unblended shirt didn't change the character of the individual; it was merely an external sign of his covenant with the Lord.

Another interesting illustration of holy behavior is found in Leviticus 27:30:

> "And all the tithe of the land, whether of the seed of the land or of the fruit of the tree, is the LORD's. It is holy to the LORD."

How could seed or fruit be holy? Only because the Lord revealed that the "tithe of the land," or 10 percent of all seed and fruit, were His and must be separated from them and separated to Him through dedication and donation.

Holiness Is Defined by the Lord and His Revelation

Biblical holiness, however, is not merely separation from the secular to the sacred, but it is *specific separation as revealed by the Lord God Himself*. For example, many "holy men" do not worship the Lord God or His Son Jesus but nevertheless seek to interface with an unseen spirit world. The Bible would describe these as antiholy men because they have devoted themselves to serve the enemies of the Lord.

Likewise, many rituals and religious practices considered by some to be the height of holiness are, in the eyes of heaven, worthless or even antiholy. For example, the Bible reveals that holy men who walk for miles on their knees to a holy temple are not performing the will of God or in any manner pleasing Him.

This principle is crucial in your pursuit of biblical holiness. The Lord sets the standards for what is holy, not man, and the Lord has revealed His standards for holiness in His Word. Look around at the confusion and distortion that runs rampant as society tells everyone to do what feels right. If you have established standards of holiness based on how you feel or think or what someone else has written outside of the Bible, these standards do not reflect biblical holiness.

Do not miss this point: Holiness is defined by the Lord, not by man. If you have invented for yourself nonbiblical practices that you deem holy, you probably have opened yourself to years of suffering and worthless behavior. This is stated clearly in Colossians 2:20–23:

> Why…do you subject yourselves to regulations—"Do not touch, do not taste, do not handle," which all concern things which perish with the using—according to the commandments and *doctrines of men?* These things indeed have

an *appearance of wisdom in self-imposed religion,* false humility, and neglect of the body, *but are of no value.*

As I have traveled around this world, my heart has been broken time after time by false, self-imposed religions and doctrines of men that cause great pain and suffering.

What then must we do to attain holiness? God Himself provides the answer in Exodus 19:5–6:

> "Now therefore, *if you will indeed obey My voice* and *keep My covenant,* then you shall be a special treasure to Me above all people; for all the earth is Mine. And you *shall be to Me* a kingdom of priests and *a holy nation."*

For people to be holy in God's eyes, they must obey His voice and keep His covenant. The Lord is the One who must define the boundaries of what is holy and what is not. A religion cannot. A denomination cannot. A local church cannot. Only the Lord God Himself has outlined the standards of true biblical holiness. Any additions or deletions to the biblical mandate must be guarded against most carefully, as they may be solely the doctrines of men.

In Jesus' lifetime, Jewish leaders taught their own particular brand of holiness. Listen to this confrontation from Matthew 15:1–3, 7–9:

> Then the scribes and Pharisees who were from Jerusalem came to Jesus, saying, "Why do Your disciples transgress the tradition of the elders? [Note: not the Bible.] For they do not wash their hands when they eat bread."

But He answered and said to them, *"Why do you also transgress the commandment of God because of your tradition?*

"Hypocrites! Well did Isaiah prophesy about you, saying: 'These people draw near to Me with their mouth, and honor Me with their lips, but their heart is far from Me...*teaching as doctrines the commandments of men.'"*

Personal preferences and standards are often presented in our churches as biblical doctrines when in reality they are not. Such commandments of men may be taught with more emotional fervor than accompanies Scripture.

The natural tendency of humanity is to allow our traditions to become more important than God's commands. In fact, we often disobey the biblical call to holiness *because of* our traditions!

In fact, the Bible expressly reveals that those who teach that certain practices are "holy" without biblical backing are actually giving heed to deceiving spirits. Read for yourself these pointed words in 1 Timothy 4:1–5:

Now the Spirit expressly says that in latter times some will depart from the faith, *giving heed to deceiving spirits and doctrines of demons,* speaking lies in hypocrisy, having their own conscience seared with a hot iron, forbidding to marry, and commanding to abstain from foods which God created to be received with thanksgiving by those who believe and know the truth. For every creature of God is good, and nothing is to be refused if it is received with thanksgiving; for it is sanctified [made holy] by the word of God and prayer.

Be extremely careful about defining the standards of true bibli-cal holiness beyond the boundaries of the Bible! Countless individuals have been greatly deceived in their pursuit of holiness through man's teachings and traditions.

External Holiness Without Internal Holiness Is Not Biblical

The final standard of biblical holiness is also revealed in Matthew 15. After calling the Pharisees hypocrites, the Lord says that their hearts are far from God. For a person to be holy, his or her heart and motives must be pure before the Lord. In other words, it is possible for a person to do something that the Bible clearly defines as holy and yet not fulfill biblical holiness. Holiness can be faked before men, but faked holiness is nothing less than unholiness!

Faked holiness is nothing less than unholiness!

When a Christian seeks holiness in his life and engages in practices that the Bible would affirm, yet permits his heart to remain aloof or even rebellious to the Lord, such behavior would be unholy—even if the behavior appears to others to be holy. For the Lord to declare something to be holy, both the habit and the heart must be separated unto the Lord. One without the other only breeds destructive unholiness.

External holiness without internal holiness breeds hypocrisy, and hypocritical holiness inevitably degenerates into the bondage of legalism.

Internal holiness without external holiness breeds emotional-ism, and emotional holiness inevitably degenerates into the bondage of fanaticism.

Biblical holiness does not drift into the dangerous waters of legalism and fanaticism, but biblical holiness defines internal and external separation by biblical standards.

May you have a clear picture of what biblical holiness is all about. And may you long for a heart and habit full of genuine, balanced holiness.

HOLINESS COMES IN STAGES

Once when my wife's parents were visiting with us, we spent hours putting together a very large and difficult jigsaw puzzle with more than 2000 pieces. Darlene Marie's parents are truly seasoned puzzle veterans. After glancing over the hundreds of pieces, I realized that this had to be one of the most difficult I had ever seen. Nothing was distinct. The sky and mountains and meadow and lake all blended together. When you picked up one piece, you soon saw that it could fit almost anywhere! But truthfully, each piece could fit in only one place.

When you come to the subject of holiness, you immediately recognize its vast scope. Holiness pieces are scattered throughout every book of the Bible! But unlike my in-laws' single picture, I am convinced that biblical holiness has a number of distinct images in its puzzle! In other words, holiness is one unified subject with several very different meanings, depending upon the biblical context.

Return for a moment to the professor's classroom. The students' different perspectives on holiness eventually separated and isolated them from one another. Each group selected a certain part of the holiness puzzle (each had a distinct and seemingly complete picture in their piece), set up walls around their particular picture, and then emotionally and denominationally defended their picture.

Obviously, when they considered their picture, there were numerous pieces—passages in the Bible—which could fit only in their picture and nowhere else. They were absolutely correct, and since their perspectives were biblical, anyone with differing views must not only be wrong, but potentially even be heretical.

No wonder holiness is so "puzzling"! After reading and studying Scriptures on holiness, I realized how very extensive the subject is. When I read certain passages, I could hear my Presbyterian friends applauding. Other passages would be favored by my Methodist and Wesleyan friends; others, my Baptist friends; and still others, my Pentecostal and charismatic friends. Depending upon which group of biblical pieces of the holiness puzzle you focus on, your understanding will likely be influenced and ultimately swayed toward a particular viewpoint.

Throughout this process, I set aside all my preconceptions. In order for this book to have biblical integrity, it must reveal what the Bible teaches, not what I may or may not believe. So I began afresh looking through passage after passage with only one question: What does this passage actually say? As best I could, I set aside those "theological boxes" with all of their boundaries and held on to only one boundary: the words and phrases and verses and paragraphs in the biblical revelation that directly related to the subject of holiness.

How frustrating! No wonder there are so very many different groups proclaiming they have the truth about holiness. My conclusion? For the most part, I believe that many are absolutely correct—they do have the truth.

They have the truth, but perhaps not the *whole* truth. For instance, were those students correct in defending their position that *trunks* mean elephants' noses? Yes. Were other students correct in defending their position that *trunks* are something found on the back of cars? Yes.

But does *trunks* always refer to the rear storage space in cars? Not at all. In other words, one can have truth without having the whole truth. *One can be fully within the boundaries of what the Bible teaches in one passage, yet outside the boundaries of what the Bible teaches in all its parts.* It is my conclusion that most of the confusion regarding this most vital subject is due to the sincere error of defining holiness by looking at only a small part of the puzzle.

Could it be that holiness indeed fits into one puzzle but also forms three different and distinct pictures within that same puzzle? Then perhaps all parts would indeed fit within one whole without contradiction!

Let's now look at three distinct yet interrelated stages of biblical holiness. You may discover, perhaps for the first time, where you stand in your personal pursuit of holiness.

Chapter 2

The Holiness of Salvation

It is not your hold of Christ that saves you,
but His hold of you.

CHARLES HADDON SPURGEON

I have three very clear goals in mind for this book. First, that your heart will be stirred so deeply by the Lord's personal call for you to be holy that you will joyfully and purposefully turn your heart toward holiness. Second, that you will understand exactly what the Bible does and doesn't teach about holiness and what to do in order to achieve the Lord's goal for you to be holy as He is holy. And third, that you will be equipped with the tools to experience holiness—tools to break you free from the bonds of unholiness in your life, tools to enable you to overcome temptations that assail you, and tools to pursue personal holiness through habits of holiness.

Instead of focusing on the holiness of God, this book focuses on *your* holiness. Instead of majoring in head knowledge, this book majors in deep life-change. Instead of pursuing theological systems, this book pursues personal transformation.

The Three Stages of Personal Holiness

When I began preparing this book in earnest, none of my "rough draft" concepts about holiness had anything remotely to do with stages of holiness. Instead, I stumbled over the idea while trying to make sense of all the many seemingly contradictory verses dealing with holiness. Each verse on holiness wasn't difficult to understand in isolation, but when two or more verses were compared and seemed to imply opposite teachings, I knew I was missing something foundational.

Finally, I paid very close attention to the tense of the verbs used in each verse. Then I arranged them into the categories of (1) holiness described in the past tense, (2) holiness described in the present tense, (3) holiness described in the future tense, and (4) holiness described in the future tense referring to the eternal state of believers.

As you can probably guess, when I compared the verses within one of these categories, they made perfect and logical sense; but when I drew comparisons between verses in different categories, things no longer seemed to fit together in any logical way.

Because this book was to focus on practical holiness in the here and now, I elected to set aside the category of verses on eternal holiness. A pattern began to emerge that suggested that there are in fact three different stages of holiness, which provided an extremely helpful framework for understanding personal holiness.

THE FIRST STAGE OF HOLINESS

Carefully read the following verse and see if you can locate the two words that are both translated from the same root word for *holiness:*

> To the church of God which is at Corinth, to those who are
> sanctified in Christ Jesus, called to be saints, with all who
> in every place call on the name of Jesus Christ our Lord.
> (1 Corinthians 1:2)

The first word here derived from the *holiness* root is *sanctified;* the second is *saints.* When you realize that the word *saints* is derived from the same root as *holiness,* this opens new vistas of understanding.

Notice that Paul describes the church at Corinth in two different ways. First, they are "*sanctified* in Christ Jesus," which means they have been made holy (or separated) in Christ through His death and resurrection. Second, they are "called to be saints."

The key here is to recognize that when Paul writes that the Corinthians are called to be saints, he doesn't mean that these Christians should grow into saints, or hopefully become saints sometime in the future. Instead, Paul means to say that the Corinthians *are* saints.

The words *to be* are italicized in modern translations of this passage because the words do not appear in the original Greek text. Let's look at this verse again as it appears in *Young's Literal Translation:*

> To the assembly of God that is in Corinth, to those sancti-
> fied in Christ Jesus, *called saints,* with all those calling upon
> the name of our Lord Jesus Christ in every place.

You see? Paul is saying to his fellow believers that they are "called saints." *Instead of being a future goal, sainthood is a present state!*

The Greek root word for *holy* is *hagios.* When *hagios* is used in noun form in the New Testament it is often translated as the word *saint,* which literally means "the separated one," or "the called-out one." Much of our confusion over the use of the word *saint* stems from the historical practice of labeling certain notable Christians saints, as in "Saint John" or "Saint Mary." Church history records that such designations of sainthood first occurred many years after the death of the apostles. Conferring "official" sainthood on an individual was not a New Testament practice, but is in reality an ecclesiastical practice.

Never does the Bible refer to a "Saint John," although some editions add this "rank" to the title of some books—for example, the

Gospel of Saint John. The fact is that the New Testament uses the word *saints* sixty-two times to describe *every single born-again believer in Jesus Christ!* If you have been born again in Him, you are already a saint, or separated one.

If you have been born again in Christ, the Bible calls you a saint.

With this in mind, we approach the first stage of holiness—the *holiness of the past tense.* At what moment did the separation take place that allows us as believers to be called separated ones? How does the first stage of holiness make you holy?

The first stage of holiness begins with your act of trusting the Lord Jesus Christ as your personal Savior. At that moment, you become a saint and are sanctified. Does that necessarily mean that your ensuing behavior reflects what is true about you?

Think about the church of Corinth for a moment. Paul referred to them as "those who are sanctified in Christ Jesus," men and women "called to be saints." Yet a couple of pages into his letter, he delivered strong words citing many of their sins, including gross immorality, lawsuits, widespread divisions, and bitter envy among others. Of all the churches mentioned in the New Testament, the Corinthian church was perhaps the most sinful and "carnal" (1 Corinthians 3:3). Yet as you read through Paul's first and second letters to this body of believers, he doesn't invite them to *become* Christians but rather to change their behavior. He does not tell them that because of their "unsaintly" behavior they can no longer be saints. Instead, he argues that because they *are* saints, they should *live as* saints. The Bible is undeniably clear: Christians are saints who may choose to live like sinners for a period of time. If Christians live like sinners, they are to be confronted and challenged to repent of their ways, to depend on the Holy Spirit and walk in holiness.

All believers have been sanctified, but not all believers live sanctified lives. Many Scripture passages support this concept, including 1 Peter 2:9–11, which underscores much of what I am seeking to make clear:

> But you *are* a chosen generation, a royal priesthood, a *holy nation,* His own special people, that you may proclaim the praises of Him who called you out of darkness into His marvelous light; who once were not a people but *are now the people of God,* who had not obtained mercy but now have obtained mercy. Beloved, I beg you as sojourners and pilgrims, *abstain from fleshly lusts* which war against the soul.

When these people had accepted Christ as their personal Savior, Peter says, they were brought "out of darkness into His marvelous light." Clearly, these had been born again and were therefore saints, having been sanctified. So why does Peter have to "beg" them to "abstain from fleshly lusts"? Because at the time of his writing, they were in fact indulging in fleshly lusts and sinning against the Lord!

The point should be clear: The sanctification that occurs because of the belief in the finished work of Jesus does not, in and of itself, equate holiness in the behavior of the believer.

So how then can we be called holy when our behavior does not reflect holiness?

When someone or something is set apart from the secular to the sacred, it is biblically called holy regardless of its nature or behavior. When the Lord selected Jerusalem and separated it to Himself as the location of David's throne, the city became holy. When the Lord selected a part of the wilderness as the place to speak to Moses and separated it to Himself, the ground became holy. Both are described as holy in Scripture not because they were changed in their appearance or nature, but because God separated them to Himself in His mind.

A person also may be described as holy in one sense without that person's nature changing. The tribe of Levi became the holy priesthood only because the Lord appointed them as His priesthood. But a quick survey of the Old Testament finds prophets repeatedly denouncing the wickedness of the priesthood. Sounds to me like the same problem the Corinthian church had hundreds of years later: saints living unsaintly lives.

You see, the essence of this first stage of holiness isn't in the change of the behavior of the person; *it's a change in the mind of God about that person.*

The sand became holy because the Lord decided to use it for His purposes. The city of Jerusalem became holy because the Lord selected it for His purposes. Likewise, the Lord separates to Himself every single person who believes in Jesus Christ as His personal Savior. At the moment of faith, the person (not his behavior) becomes holy, a saint in the eyes of God, supernaturally separated to Himself.

HOW TO BECOME A SAINT

Becoming a saint is an instantaneous event rather than a gradual progression toward godliness. In order to deepen our understanding of this remarkable fact, let's explore the roles of the Holy Spirit, Jesus Christ, and the believer in this miraculous transformation called the new birth.

The Role of the Holy Spirit

The Holy Spirit is the agent through which this first stage of sanctification is instituted. Second Thessalonians 2:13 is most helpful in understanding this:

> We are bound to give thanks to God always for you, brethren beloved by the Lord, because God from the beginning chose you for salvation *through sanctification by the Spirit* and belief in the truth.

At the moment of saving faith, the Holy Spirit sets us apart unto God. The Holy Spirit regenerates us so that we become born again (see John 3:3–8); He seals us until the day of redemption (see Ephesians 4:30); He is sent forth into our hearts by the Father (see Galatians 4:6); He indwells us (see Romans 8:11); He baptizes us into the body of Christ (see 1 Corinthians 12:13); He gives us spiritual gifts (see 1 Corinthians 12:7, 11, 18); and He bears spiritual fruit in our lives (see Galatians 5:22).

This incredible process of first-stage sanctification is primarily the work of the Holy Spirit. All these blessings are granted instantaneously to the believer by the sanctifying work of the Spirit, whether the believer knows it or not. Notice that the Spirit does every one of these works, not the believer.

The Role of the Father and the Son

The work of sanctification, or becoming a saint, is accomplished by the Holy Spirit on the basis of the work of salvation accomplished by the Lord Jesus Christ. This is underscored in 1 Corinthians 6:11: "You were washed, but you were sanctified, but you were justified in the name of the Lord Jesus and by the Spirit of our God."

A person is sanctified and justified only by means of the Lord Jesus. If Jesus had not finished His work, then the Spirit couldn't do His. The author of Hebrews offers profound insight into this amazing work of Christ:

By that will [the work of the Father in salvation] we have been sanctified through the offering of the body of Jesus Christ once for all. But this Man, after He had offered one sacrifice for sins forever, sat down at the right hand of God, from that time waiting till His enemies are made His footstool. (Hebrews 10:10, 12–13)

Such a profound statement in so few words. A human being can be accepted by God and separated to Him for His purposes only because of the "once for all" sacrifice of Jesus. Christ died once—for all sins, for all people, for all time.

God considers all mankind to be on one side or the other. Before Him, a person is either unholy or holy. If a person is unholy, he is separated from God; if a person is holy, then he is separated to God. Unholy men and women are separated from God because of their sin in rebellion against God and their rejection of the sacrifice of Jesus. The penalty for such disobedience against God is the death penalty, including both physical death and eternal death in hell.

When Christ died, He offered His life as full payment for our sins. Unless Christ had paid for the sins of mankind, all of us would be headed for eternal damnation. No court of appeal. No getting off on a technicality. No Get-Out-of-Hell-Free card. But out of grace and mercy and love, the Father sent His only begotten Son to die so that you and I may live forever with Him.

The Role of the Believer

Christ's work finished everything necessary for your salvation; the Spirit's work applies Christ's work to you. So what is the work you must do to be saved?

Absolutely nothing! There is no unfinished work remaining for you to do.

Ephesians 2:8–9 captures the essence of the "no work" wonder of your salvation: "For by grace you have been saved through faith, and that not of yourselves; it is the gift of God, not of works, lest anyone should boast."

The Bible can't be any clearer than that, can it? Salvation is not given to you because of who you are or what you've done. Salvation can't be something you do, because Christ did it. Salvation can't be a work you achieve, because Christ already achieved it.

And because your works have nothing to do with completing Christ's work, never again let yourself become confused about these two major issues: first, the oft-mistaken notion that *I must begin doing "good works" in order to be saved;* and second, the idea that *I must stop doing "bad works" in order to be saved.*

Since Christ's death on the cross was the only "work" God the Father would accept as payment for your sins, your good works are totally irrelevant in this regard. From the beginning, even in the Garden of Eden, God said the punishment for disobedience is the death penalty. Our good works may be acceptable restitution for breaking the speed limit or public drunkenness; but even in our courts, public service doesn't count toward the death penalty, no matter how many hours are served or how difficult the work.

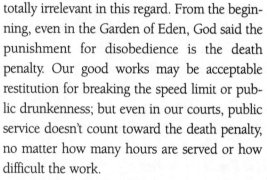

Public service doesn't count toward the death penalty, no matter how many hours you serve.

"Bad works" is merely another way of describing sin. Since Christ's death on the cross already paid for every single sin you have committed or will ever commit, stopping your sin won't change anything regarding your salvation. Whether you sin tomorrow or not you will not change the finished work of Christ two thousand years ago!

Therefore, regarding your salvation, you should feel entirely helpless. No matter where you turn, there's nothing you can do to fix the problem. Not by trying harder and doing more good things. Not by trying harder and avoiding more bad things. You can't do one single thing to fix the problem of your sin or earn forgiveness from God.

So what must you do to be saved? Once again: Absolutely nothing! Well then, let me help you rephrase the question: "Since I am a sinner and have willfully disobeyed God and rightly earned the eternal death penalty, how can I connect with what Christ did for me on the cross and know God's forgiveness and be given eternal life?"

The beloved apostle John had your question in mind when he wrote, "But as many as *received Him,* to them He gave the right to become children of God, to those *who believe in His name*" (John 1:12).

Salvation is a free gift, offered to all who will accept. Because there's absolutely, unequivocally nothing you can do, because Jesus has absolutely and unequivocally finished everything for you, all that's left is merely to *believe* that He did it all for you and receive Him as your Savior.

Nothing more will work. And nothing less will work.

THE GIFT OF SALVATION

Sound simple? Like merely reaching out your hand and accepting a gift being offered to you? It is.

Paul said it this way to the church at Ephesus: "For by grace you have been saved through faith, and that not of yourselves; it is the gift of God" (Ephesians 2:8).

Paul and Silas said it this way to the Philippian jailer: "Believe on the Lord Jesus Christ, and you will be saved" (Acts 16:31).

Jesus said it this way to Nicodemus: "For God so loved the world that He gave His only begotten Son, that whoever believes in Him should not perish but have everlasting life" (John 3:16).

So, my friend, how many more must say it before you realize that your salvation is fully the work of Christ and requires only your faith in His finished work on the cross? He shed His precious blood as full and complete payment for the death penalty for your sins.

If you have never knelt before the King of glory and received His matchless gift of eternal life, then now may be your time to kneel and say to Him with all of your heart:

> *Lord, I kneel in humility, confessing that I am a sinner*
> *and rightly deserve the death penalty You have declared*
> *as just payment for all who sin against You.*
> *I confess that nothing I can do is able to pay*
> *for my sins except my physical and eternal death.*
> *I believe Christ died and was resurrected for me,*
> *and I receive His wonderful gift of eternal life.*
> *I hereby accept the Lord Jesus Christ as my Savior.*
> *In Jesus' name, amen.*

If you've just received God's gift of salvation, then you are truly born again and God calls you holy!

Now let's move onward and upward to the second stage of holiness.

Chapter 3

Presenting Yourself to God

The greatness of a man's power is the measure of his surrender.
WILLIAM BOOTH

y heart was pounding and sweat dripped down my back. The intensity of the past thirty-five minutes of speaking had just about worn me out. The Lord had moved mightily in the stadium, and now thousands of men streamed forward in genuine repentance and with heartfelt recommitment.

Now I was being ushered down a corridor in the bowels of the stadium to a little room for a radio interview. I'll never forget the moment that door opened, revealing *seven* radio microphones all pointed directly at me like spears in a hostile jungle. Someone asked, "Dr. Wilkinson, you don't actually believe those men are going to be changed, do you? We all know that men don't change overnight just by making an emotional decision in public."

"That's a good question," I ventured. "Are you married?"

"What difference does *that* make?" the reporter answered defensively. "But yes, I am married."

Without breaking eye contact, I said, "When you got married, did you come forward? And at that moment, were you as emotional as most guys are when they get married?"

His stance softened just a tad. "I suppose so…but so what?"

"When you came forward that day and made that commitment, would you say that decision changed the rest of your life?"

Can a single decision change a person's life? Of course! Not only can a decision change your life, but if you looked back over your life, you would find that your path has been determined precisely by the decisions you've made, many of them filled with emotion. Many a decision has resulted in a turning point—a moment that influenced your future, shaped your career, molded your family, and even determined your eternal destiny. Never underestimate the significance of the important decisions you make. They change your life.

Soon I'm going to invite you to make a decision that, as you will see, will change your life forever.

THE SECOND STAGE OF HOLINESS

In reading the Word of God, have you ever stumbled onto something you already knew, but rediscovered it in an entirely new way? That happened to me as I studied anew what the New Testament had to say about holiness. I stumbled onto Romans 12:1, an old friend for many years. My first inclination was to pass it over in search of a new and yet unconsidered idea; but fortunately I chose to amble down this familiar path.

Much to my surprise, Romans 12:1 led me to a distinct second stage of holiness that logically and biblically follows the first stage. Consider the verse:

> I beseech you therefore, brethren, by the mercies of God, that you present your bodies a living sacrifice, *holy,* acceptable to God, which is your reasonable service.

As you can see, the holiness Paul speaks of here has nothing to do with becoming a believer in Jesus Christ. Paul is talking about presenting your body as a living sacrifice to God, an action that *follows* the decision to become a Christian. This second stage of holiness requires a believer to *separate himself* to the Lord.

Paul is calling for a commitment to God—distinct from the decision to put our faith in Christ—that moves the believer down the path toward personal holiness. This is significant in the pursuit of practical holiness, and the recorded experiences of Christian leaders throughout church history bear witness to the strategic significance of this second stage.

Romans 12:1 invites believers to take the next step after salvation (a step sometimes taken the very moment after a person is born again). But in thirty years of ministry around the world, I have discovered only a small percentage of Christians who have done this. Unless you understand and break through to this second stage, you will find yourself repeatedly floundering in your pursuit of personal holiness.

A ROYAL INVITATION

First, let's explore the issue of "presenting" ourselves to God. There are really three parts to this: an invitation, a motivation, and a presentation ceremony in which a believer decides to present him- or herself fully to the Lord. As we look at what Scripture has to say about presentation, it is my prayer you will decide to join the ranks of those who understand and choose to make a personal presentation.

The Request to Present Yourself Is Not a Command but an Invitation

The phrase "I beseech you therefore" sets the tone for the rest of the verse. Instead of commanding, Paul pleads with his audience to take this action. Whenever you plead with a person, you are seeking to touch his or her heart and mind. Paul recognizes that for the presentation of oneself to God to be meaningful and life-changing, one's heart must be in it.

The Invitation to Present Yourself Is Offered to Born-Again Christians

Romans is by many accounts the most profound book in the New Testament. Paul outlines the major doctrines of the Christian faith and presents them in a logical, compelling fashion unique in Scripture. But Romans is unmistakably written to Christians, not to seekers or unbelievers.

Romans 1:8 tells us Paul's readers are saints whose faith "is spoken of throughout the whole world." It is therefore no mistake that Romans 12:1 is written to the believer in Jesus Christ, because it is impossible for a nonbeliever to do what this verse teaches.

If a person who is not a saint seeks to devote himself to the Lord, the Lord is unable to receive him. His presentation as a living sacrifice cannot be holy or acceptable to God. Why? Because as we have seen, the only valid and acceptable approach to God is through the shed blood of Jesus Christ. When individuals who have not believed in Christ seek to devote themselves to God, they are seeking to find favor with God through an act of personal sacrifice rather than through Christ's act of sacrifice.

Salvation Does Not Require Dedication

God is very clear—salvation does not exist except through the death and resurrection of Jesus Christ. What must you do in addition to genuinely believing in Christ? Must you consecrate yourself to Him in any way in order to be saved? No. The Bible is clear: "Believe on the Lord Jesus Christ, and you will be saved" (Acts 16:31).

Belief in a person and devotion to that person are different things. I can believe in a person without devoting my life to him. Although I have heard and read many arguments in favor of adding things to "Believe on the Lord Jesus Christ, and you will be saved," the Bible teaches that *nothing* will save anyone except genuine faith in Christ. Adding any other condition is unbiblical.

Consecration occurs when a Christian decides of his own free will to dedicate himself to Christ in a deep and meaningful way; but consecration is not required in order to experience salvation. *In fact, because Romans 12:1 was written to Christians who had been saved anywhere from days to more than twenty years, clearly an extensive period of time may pass between the decision to trust Christ as Savior and the later decision to devote oneself totally to God.* Or it may never occur! Paul does not warn that believers will lose their salvation if they never dedicate their lives to the Lord.

The concept of discipleship must be separated as a distinct

truth from salvation, or the gospel is tragically blurred. Consider carefully these words by Oswald Chambers:

> Discipleship and salvation are two different things: a disciple is one who, realizing the meaning of the atonement, deliberately gives himself up to Jesus Christ in unspeakable gratitude. Jesus invites us to take up our cross and follow Him daily. We are at perfect liberty to toss our spiritual heads and say, "No, thank you; that's a bit too stern for me," and the Lord will never say a word. We can do exactly what we like. He will never plead, but the opportunity is there to live a life that God rewards.

WHY PRESENT MYSELF TO THE LORD?

Have you ever fully and completely consecrated yourself to the Lord? The Lord encourages His children to present themselves to Him as living sacrifices, and my prayer is that He will use this book to move you to make this important commitment.

Like many in the church today, Matthew labored on a spiritual merry-go-round—around and around he went, but without progressing any further in his spiritual life. He had grown steadily as a new Christian but eventually floundered, hit a plateau, and began a slow decline. We met on a Friday night, and he wanted to know if I could help him.

As we talked, his problem soon became clear: Matthew had never come to the place in his life where he dedicated himself without reservation to the Lord. This logjam in his heart inevitably bred frustration, confusion, and spiritual decline. Because he had elected not to put Christ first in every area of his life, Matthew was simply unable to enjoy sustained victory in his life.

He told me that although he wanted to dedicate his life to the Lord, every time he tried, he ended up slamming on his brakes and running into a proverbial ditch. With a heavy sigh of resignation, Matthew confessed he only hoped to lick this problem someday.

I hope you haven't fallen into the trap of thinking that the spiritual life is just too complicated, too difficult, too haphazard, and so you just drift rudderless on the ocean, hoping things will change. But if you suffer from the same malady as Matthew, the Bible offers specific help and motivation—a cure for the common life.

MOTIVATION FOR DEDICATION

As Romans 12:1 is the key passage on presenting yourself as a living sacrifice, the answer may lie right at our fingertips. How did the apostle Paul encourage the church at Rome to consecrate themselves? "I beseech you therefore, brethren, *by the mercies of God,* that you present your bodies a living sacrifice."

Whereas the world tells us that the power is within each of us to "just do it," God knows that we cannot sufficiently motivate ourselves to deny the flesh and pursue holiness on a daily basis. We need something more to spur us to action. According to Paul, our motivation to dedicate ourselves to the Lord is found in the mercies of God. We are not expected to pursue holiness merely out of a sense of responsibility or duty but instead out of a sense of appreciation. Paul isn't trying to motivate us by promising a reward of some kind or by threatening discipline or pain. He isn't relying on some inbred sense of moral responsibility. The motivation to give yourself to God is solely based upon what God has done for you. As

C. T. Studd once said, "If Jesus Christ is God and died for me, then no sacrifice can be too great for me to make for Him."

I asked our friend Matthew, "What are some of the things the Lord has done for you that mean the most to you?" He could only think of two before he began to struggle, and then he became uncomfortable, sensing that he should obviously know many more. But he didn't. Why? Because it never fails: Christians who struggle to dedicate themselves also struggle to recall the many mercies of God in their lives.

Give yourself to God because of what God has done for you.

When I meet someone who is struggling to commit themselves to the Lord, I automatically know that his "mercies memory bank" is low on deposits. But when I ask a highly consecrated individual about what the Lord has done for him, I am always deeply touched by a flood of personal illustrations.

So what was the clear biblical answer to Matthew's predicament? Load his memory bank with the mercies of God! Paul used this same approach, filling to overflowing his readers' memory banks and touching their emotional strings with the mercies of God. Then and only then did he request that they dedicate themselves to the Lord.

I believe the entire book of Romans builds to this very point. After salvation—remember, Paul wrote this book to Christians—the next most strategic step in spiritual growth is the presentation of one's life. What would motivate an entire church to do such a remarkable thing? Only a deep and comprehensive understanding of what God has done for them.

In verse after verse of the first eleven chapters of Romans, Paul lays out the incredible mercies of God in rapid and logical fashion, so that the transitional word *therefore* in Romans 12:1 summarizes not the last few verses, but the entire book up to that point. Everything builds to Romans 12:1, and all that follows is a result of the personal presentation as a living sacrifice.

But why does the Lord want you to choose to present yourself as a living sacrifice? What is to be gained by such an act? The answer to this question once again demonstrates the incredible grace of the Lord. Look what is true about you even *before* you present yourself to the Lord:

> Do you not know that your body is the temple of the Holy Spirit who is in you, whom you have from God, and you are not your own? For you were bought at a price; therefore glorify God in your body and in your spirit, which are God's. (1 Corinthians 6:19–20)

The Lord Himself took ownership of your body from the moment you trusted Christ! His death was the price tag for the purchase of your life. Therefore, you are not your own, but you may have been living as if you were your own up to this point.

Why then didn't Paul choose to announce the truth that we are already God's and simply instruct us that we had better live that way? Because the Lord always seeks the voluntary dedication of His children. He knows that unless our hearts are committed, our actions will become uncommitted. So, even though you and I already belong to the Lord, He invites us to present ourselves to Him as a living sacrifice, abandoning to Him all rights to ourselves.

The Next Logical Step

Although the presentation of one's life can be a very emotional time, the root of the action must also be reasonable and logical to the person. Because Romans 12:1 says that your act of consecration is "your reasonable service," the act of releasing yourself to the Lord should be the most logical and mentally defensible thing you will ever do. If you dedicate yourself to the Lord in a moment of fleeting emotion rather than after careful consideration, you will find it difficult to reconcile yourself to your action the next day and the day after that.

In the high Rocky Mountains one day, I spent some time with a businessman from the Colorado Springs area. Like Matthew, this man sought spiritual breakthrough but was frustrated because he had never consecrated himself to God. For two hours, I gently but relentlessly probed his heart, his knowledge of the Word, and his awareness of the Lord's personal involvement in his life. The more his eyes were opened to the truth of the Lord's mercies, the more he softened.

Issue by issue, we dealt with his hidden hardness of heart toward God due to his misunderstanding of the truth. His hardness soon turned to confession and praise and adoration. Together we scaled the incredible mercies of God's redemption, propitiation, reconciliation, adoption, and gift of the Holy Spirit.

Finally, something broke deep in his heart and he fell on his knees. "Lord, how can I remain away from You? How I have suffered by saying no to You while saying yes to me. How foolish I have been to fight You when You have fought for me and sacrificed Your Son for me. Is there any other besides You who is worthy of giving my life to? Lord, I humble myself before You and offer myself up to You—a living sacrifice!"

You see, friend, when you see the whole truth about the Lord and His love and care and compassions and loyalty for you, the only logical step is to immediately and fully commit yourself into His loving arms.

NURTURED BY THE BELIEVER AND THE CHURCH

In Matthew's case, I gave him an assignment in order to load his memory bank with the truth of the Lord's mercies with the hopes of setting his heart free. I asked him to read Romans 1–11, Ephesians 1–3, and Colossians 1–2 and list on a couple of sheets everything the Lord had done for him personally. We met the next evening around nine at the conference center's frozen yogurt stand. Matthew brought numerous sheets crumpled around the edges. When I first saw him, I noticed his eyes had softened and his demeanor had become more peaceful. "Well, Matthew, what did you find?"

"I had no idea!" he said. "I mean, where have I been all these years as a Christian? Just look at this list, and I didn't have time to finish all the chapters. The Lord is just incredible!"

"So tell me about what's on your list." Off he went, listing the correct information but clearly not yet embracing the truth with his heart. "Slow down, Matt, and let your heart interpret the truth in your head. How do you emotionally feel, for instance, about God adopting you as His son?"

That was the cork I was searching for. Matthew's eyes overflowed with tears that had been trapped all of his Christian life. The goodness of God hit the fear of Matthew's heart and overwhelmed him. Soon Matthew was sobbing, his heart broken for the first time with the personal love the Lord had for him. Guess what happened that night under the tall trees of northern California? Heaven shouted for joy as another struggling believer became a living sacrifice.

If I sense my own personal devotion is waning, what do I do? Return to the mercies of the Lord in the Scriptures and stir up my heart with the truth. I pull out my personal journal and read of His many mercies in my life. I open my prayer journal and slowly read through the hundreds of specific answers to prayer I have recorded in the past few years. I open my heart and flood the throne of heaven with my fervent praise and adoration. I won't stop until my consecration is completely restored. No matter how far my heart may have strayed, I know with full assurance that my heart must be mastered—and will be mastered—until it is fully and joyfully submissive to the Lord of glory!

Unfortunately, however, too many of us don't know what to do with our hearts. I pray that at this very moment you will rise up and review the files in your mind marked "mercies of God" and pluck the strings of your heart until it plays in beautiful harmony with the melodies of heaven.

Although this book isn't specifically written to pastors and Christian leaders, I feel constrained to say that with rare exception, I have found God's church lacking in teaching on biblical consecration. Early in the twentieth century, the Lord's shepherds openly challenged their flocks to dedicate themselves to the Lord and commit to a life of holiness. Now it is seldom preached from the pulpit. And how the church has suffered because of it! Pastors, we in leadership need to rise up and fulfill our calling with powerful, anointed preaching that God uses to change lives!

THIS IS YOUR LIFE!

So how do we "present" our lives to God? And what does it mean to be a living sacrifice? Let's take a closer look at what Paul is really saying in Romans 12:1.

The Meaning of Present

The word *present* as used in Romans 12:1 carries with it both a general and specific meaning. Generally, the word means "to offer," or "to bring." More specifically, Greek scholars point out that the word also was used to describe the person who presents a lamb to the priest. Here, Paul is exhorting us to bring ourselves as lambs to the heavenly High Priest.

In the Gospel of Luke, *present* is used to describe what Joseph and Mary did with the infant Jesus in the temple:

> Now when the days of her purification according to the law
> of Moses were completed, they brought Him to Jerusalem
> *to present Him to the Lord* (as it is written in the law of the
> Lord, "Every male who opens the womb shall be *called holy
> to the* LORD"). (Luke 2:22–23)

This illustrates the concept of presentation of a person to God in such a way that it was "holy to the Lord." When Joseph and Mary presented Jesus to the Lord, they offered Him back to the Lord and dedicated Him to the Lord's purposes. Believing parents can offer their children to the Lord as living sacrifices through infant dedication, with the realization of the Lord's pleasure. However, the child must later come to know Christ and then choose to devote him- or herself fully to the Lord.

The Meaning of a Living Sacrifice

Paul's call to the believer to make himself a "living sacrifice" must have shaken his first-century readers. Paul selected, under divine inspiration, an incredibly graphic picture of how completely the Lord sought the life of the believer.

Under the old covenant, sacrificial animals were to be presented alive, healthy, and without blemish, or the Lord would not accept them. Now, instead of an animal, the believer is called to bring *himself* as the sacrifice and then offer himself to God.

This probably brought to mind the only other human sacrifice requested by God in the Bible: Abraham's sacrifice of his beloved son Isaac. As Abraham brought down his knife to slay his son, an angel of the Lord stopped him, saying, "Do not lay your hand on the lad, or do anything to him; for now I know that you fear God, since you have not withheld your son, your only son, from Me" (Genesis 22:12). The Lord brought Abraham to a crisis of consecration. Who would Abraham choose to be first in his life: his son or his God?

Who will be first in your life—you or your Savior?

Now, instead of your son, the Lord requests your very own life. Once again, the underlying issue is this: Who will be number one in your life, you or your Savior?

Another distinction from the old covenant sacrifice lies in what makes the sacrifice valuable. In an Old Testament sacrifice, the animal had value only at the very moment it died. Its life had no merit; its dead body had no merit. The act of dying provided the atoning payment for man's sin.

In contrast, the real value of our consecration is not the moment of "dying," but rather our life after we have dedicated ourselves to live for God. The contrast is unmistakable. The believer dies to himself in order to live effectively for the Lord.

The Meaning of Holy

As seen in Romans 12:1, consecration of one's life to the Lord occurs in the heart and mind of the believer as he separates himself wholly unto the Lord as His servant. I personally believe that this presentation is similar to the decision to follow Christ as a disciple and not just as a believer.

Luke 14 presents conditions for discipleship which have absolutely nothing to do with eternal salvation but everything to do with obedience and service:

> "If anyone comes to Me and does not hate his father and mother, wife and children, brothers and sisters, yes, and his own life also, he cannot be My disciple. And whoever does not bear his cross and come after Me cannot be My disciple…. Whoever of you does not forsake all that he has cannot be My disciple." (Luke 14:26–27, 33)

In the midst of these powerful verses, the Lord exhorts those who are considering whether to become one of His disciples to carefully count the costs which one must pay to be a disciple. Both Luke 14 and Romans 12 present an invitation to make a major life decision followed by actions that must be carefully considered as they carry lifelong consequences.

Because of the seriousness and consequences of this decision, many who make it experience intense emotion, almost spiritual birth pangs. This commitment to the Lord is often so dramatic and deep that numerous people seem to misinterpret what exactly happened. Unfortunately, because some teach that until you consecrate yourself you cannot be saved, numerous adult believers incorrectly interpret this act of consecration and discipleship. I once taught an in-depth series that outlined the stages all believers go through en route to full conformity to Jesus Christ. Consecration is one of those stages, and over half of the conference participants kneeled and presented themselves to the Lord.

After this happened, I warned the audience not to think that this act had anything to do with their eternal salvation. Many of these middle-aged adults accepted Christ as their personal Savior as children, but they didn't give themselves fully to the Lord until their thirties, forties, or fifties. When the consecration is very intense and emotional, many people are tempted to "rewrite" their spiritual lives and erase their true conversion experience due to the depth of their consecration.

If as a child you chose of your own free will to accept Jesus Christ as your personal Savior and genuinely believed that He died for your sins and that only through His death and resurrection could you be saved, then you received eternal life at that very moment! Don't ever forget that truth, and don't ever allow anyone to confuse you: *Salvation comes only through the sacrifice of Christ, and consecration comes only through the sacrifice of yourself to Christ.*

The Meaning of "Acceptable to God"

The last phrase in Romans 12:1 is among the most inspiring in the Bible. How can you be sure that the Lord will accept your sacrifice? I'll never forget counseling a young woman who desperately sought to devote herself to the Lord but who, because of a long history of sexual immorality when she was young, was sure that God couldn't accept her. How wonderful it was to reveal the Lord's precommitment to her! In Romans 12:1, the Lord tells us that all who would present themselves to Him as a living sacrifice would be deemed acceptable!

So must a person change all his behavior in order to become a living sacrifice? No. Romans 12:1 invites the believer to separate himself to the Lord as a living sacrifice. Romans 12:2 then focuses on the ensuing actions of obedience, godliness, and service: "And do not be conformed to this world, but be transformed by the renewing of your mind, that you may prove what is that good and acceptable and perfect will of God." The order is so very clear: Present yourself to the Lord first, and then don't be conformed to the world but be transformed by the renewing of your mind. The order isn't "Don't be conformed to this world but be transformed by the renewing of your mind, and then, by the mercies of God, present yourself as a living sacrifice."

THE CEREMONY OF CONSECRATION

This chapter must draw to a close with a question: Will you now present yourself as a living sacrifice to the Lord? If so, set aside these next few moments as "holy" and dedicate them to the Lord. Set aside the place where you are seated as "holy ground" to undertake eternal business with God.

I wish I could be with you at this moment, by your side, for I would kneel with you and lead you through the following prayer. If your heart beckons you to meet heaven's request, please kneel at this time with this book in your hands and pray this prayer with me:

Heavenly Father, I hereby kneel in humility
before Your throne.
I come into Your presence of my
own free will to be here with You.
You are the most gracious and loving Person in the universe.
Your kindness to me has no boundaries or limits.
Your lovingkindness guides everything You do toward me.
Your mercies are new every morning.
Great is Thy faithfulness!
Your love sent Jesus Christ to die in my
place and give me eternal life.
I now respond to Your love and give myself
to You in this solemn moment.
Forgive me for taking so long to come to
this point of total consecration.
I hereby lift myself up to Your altar and present
myself to You as a living sacrifice.
I consecrate and dedicate myself to You for the rest of my life.
Thank You for accepting this sincere presentation.
In Jesus' name, amen.

Is this act truly a life-changing moment for Christians? I recently received a letter from a man who had watched a video series I produced on this subject. My heart rejoiced when I read this:

> When you asked if I had responded to the Lord by giving my life totally to Him and to die to myself while I am still living, it caused me to feel a thrill of anticipation. I'm sure the Spirit leaped inside me at that thought, for I couldn't wait to offer myself as a living sacrifice. It happened at 7:00 A.M., on March 18, on the floor of my family room. Praise our Lord! I now belong totally to Him!

Believer, your floor awaits your knees, and your Father awaits your life. Experience the incredible joy of giving your life away to the One who gave His life for you.

Chapter 4

I Want to Be More Like Christ

It is time for us Christians to face up to our responsibility for holiness.
Too often we say we are "defeated" by this or that sin. No, we are not
defeated; we are simply disobedient. It might be well if we stopped using
the terms "victory" and "defeat" to describe our progress in holiness.
Rather we should use the terms "obedience" and "disobedience."

JERRY BRIDGES

Every night after dinner, we met around the campfire under the incredibly beautiful wilderness sky. A rare contentment filled our lives those days as all of us once again became adventurous boys camping out along remote rivers and fishing from dawn to dusk for those incomparable salmon trophies. Our guide knew every bend and twist in the swirling waters and somehow knew where the secret pockets lay just waiting for our all-too-anxious lures.

As twenty close friends, we spent an unforgettable week fishing; but times we shared around the campfire became the real trophy memories. The Bible was opened and our hearts melted under the nightly movements of the Holy Spirit. Nary a man left for his bedroll who hadn't been touched—and changed. One night I knew it was time to deal with some of the deepest struggles that men face with an open, transparent, and direct approach.

I asked these men if any of them had experienced a real breakthrough in one part of their life—an area where they used to sin big-time, but sin no longer. Silence filled the clearing until someone threw a fresh log on the fire, shooting sparks upward like tiny rockets. Then one of the men sitting at the top of the circle said, "Well, I guess I can begin. I used to love money. I mean *really love money*. Money ruled my life—and it nearly destroyed my family and children. I was obsessed. Then God began breaking through about the fact that money was my god and I worshiped it more than Him. For about six months the Lord brought me through the wringer until I finally broke and confessed my heart of covetousness. Now I don't love money anymore. In fact, now I love to give money away! I can honestly say that I'm a different person than I used to be. I don't love money anymore. It's great!"

Many heads nodded around that circle. I knew this man well on both sides of this victory, and he was genuinely a different man. His family couldn't be any happier! But as I looked around that circle, I watched at least six men looking down at the fire nearly the whole time he shared. Why? I knew all of them well, and none of those six could yet say they were free from the love of money. One of those men was embroiled in money-related difficulties that very week, and we had had a couple of deep and intense conversations.

Then a man whom the others respected spoke up. "Well, this might surprise you, but for years I was hooked on pornography of one kind or another. To say that I was addicted would almost be an understatement. Now I was never actually physically unfaithful to my wife with another woman, but I lived in sexual bondage and infidelity through magazines, videos, cable—you know what I mean." More than a few heads nodded, although not many were breathing at this point. Such honesty and transparency demand one's fullest attention, don't they?

"Nearly ten years ago, the Lord and I had it out. I desperately wanted freedom from this bondage. I couldn't pray; I couldn't read my Bible much because it always made me feel guilty; and every time I served the Lord at church I felt like a huge hypocrite. I started confessing my sins to the Lord and decided I couldn't do it alone. So I told everything—and I mean everything—to two of my best buds, and they held me accountable!

"But guys..." He became very quiet and solemnly looked into the eyes of each man, one at a time around that circle. "Today, I am free from this sexual perversion! I haven't sinned in this area for almost ten years! You talk about freedom in Christ! Can you imagine what this did in my marriage and in my sex life with my wife?" Then he began laughing, a laugh from deep down inside. "I'm free! And if you are in bondage, you too can be free! Just come to see me later or get in my boat tomorrow, and I'll help you get started!"

Then after some remarkable discussion, I said, "Men, that's exactly what the Christian life is all about! It's the utter joy of looking back over your shoulder and honestly saying to yourself, 'I used to commit this sin, but now I don't; I walk in holiness in that area.' If you have been growing in holiness in your life, you should be able to identify at least one major area of sin that no longer is a constant struggle for you. That's what the work of Christ has provided for all of us—the promise of progressive holiness! And next year when we see each other, perhaps there will be one or two more areas where you have progressed to complete victory. How many of you could name at least one major area in your life that used to be unholy but now is holy?" About twelve of the twenty men raised their hands while the rest found the fire too intensely interesting.

Let's focus now on the third stage of holiness—progressive holiness. This means becoming more like Christ year after year—less unholy and more holy.

STAGE THREE: PROGRESSIVE HOLINESS

Progressive holiness means that Christians grow from one level of holiness to a greater level, while lessening their practice of unholiness. Progressive holiness means you can and should continually move forward and upward in your spiritual life, becoming more like Christ.

This stage of holiness actually begins at the moment of your salvation and concludes with the moment of your physical death. In that window of time, whether a few moments or a hundred years, progressive holiness is to be one of your life's chief goals and passions. How you sow your life will result in what you reap, whether holiness or unholiness.

At the moment of salvation, we are all equally holy in the Lord's sight because He sets us apart as holy. Our character is not yet Christlike, nor is our conduct completely Christlike. Progressive holiness means that I continue to become more and more Christlike in my character and conduct. To the degree that I am Christlike in these two areas, the Lord would characterize me as holy in my life.

How much we become holy as He is holy depends on our response to the Lord's work in our life. God works continuously to conform us to His Son. Any lack of holiness in our lives is not due to His failure but ours; any lack of conformity is not due to His lack of participation but to our resistance. In the life of the believer, a lack of holiness is always due to resistance and rebellion against the Lord's call and work in that person's life.

Progressive holiness in your life will be objectively seen and noticed by you and by others. As your conduct changes, you will notice that you don't behave the way you used to—and shouldn't! As your character changes, your motives and casual responses will be transformed. Instead of responding with anger, you will find yourself responding with patience and self-control. Instead of succumbing to selfishness, you will put others ahead of yourself, caring for them even before yourself. Instead of gossiping and criticizing, you will guard your tongue and speak only that which edifies and builds up. Instead of bondage to immorality, you will live in sexual fidelity and loyalty. Those changes reflect transitions from works of the flesh to fruit of the spirit; and as you grow in holiness, your life will transform before your eyes into the image of Christ.

> *You will reap what you sow, whether holiness or unholiness.*

Paul wrote, "Let us cleanse ourselves from all filthiness of the flesh and spirit, *perfecting holiness* in the fear of God" (2 Corinthians 7:1). Note that this kind of holiness requires that we "cleanse ourselves." Cleansing is an absolute requirement! Note also, however, that Paul reveals true holiness isn't a completed process but one which requires ongoing perfecting. The Greek word translated as *perfecting* means to properly bring to an end, to finish, to complete. Holiness has been birthed in the heart at conversion, and Paul exhorts believers to make every effort to complete it in all of its parts. This third stage of holiness must be progressive and continue throughout all of your converted life. You are holy; you are becoming more holy; and you will ultimately become holy like Christ upon your death.

MISCONCEPTIONS OF HOLINESS

Even as I typed these words on my trusty laptop, I paused and prayed for you, friend, that the Holy Spirit would open your eyes to the biblical truths of personal holiness. The subject of holiness is largely misunderstood among Christians, many of whom suffer terrible bondage and live from defeat to defeat instead of from victory to victory.

Late one evening after an extensive and demanding meeting in the Midwest, I walked to my car in the brisk evening air, looking forward to a much-needed night of rest. Then I saw someone in the bright moonlight. His head hung low and his shoulders sagged with such discouragement that my heart went out to this man, even before I could see who he was. As it turned out, this was a dignified church statesman who at seventy-two years of age served the Lord with such intense sacrifice and noble leadership that he had garnered the respect of all who knew him.

We stopped and greeted one another and chatted briefly about the conference. Then I gently said, "My friend, I sense the Lord may have put us together on this dark corner for an important reason. Is there any way I can be of service to you? Will you share your heart with me?"

He breathed a sigh of heaviness. After a few awkward moments, he shared his grievous burden. Just a few hours earlier at dinner, a young woman had bent down in front of him to pick up her dropped fork and, unfortunately, her blouse was very revealing. My respected friend confessed that he had given in to lustful thoughts about her. "Bruce, how could I have done that? I sinned with lust! This proves that I am not a true believer of Jesus. Unfortunately, I did this once before about three years ago. I am a terrible sinner! And I've already consecrated my life to the Lord; how could I have ever done this?" Then he began to shake his head back and forth. "Now I know that I will never be saved!"

My heart broke for my brother. If ever there was a true born-again believer who walked in holiness and served the Lord sacrificially and courageously, it was this man. Yet he was convinced that because of his sin, he couldn't be saved. Emotional trauma and internal fear plagued a mature Christian leader, all because of a deep confusion regarding salvation and sanctification. We spoke for another thirty minutes about the difference between the salvation of his soul and the perfection of his holiness. We prayed together in the twilight,

Many live from defeat to defeat instead of from victory to victory.

and he confessed his sin of lust and emotional disloyalty to his wife. Then, amazingly, for the first time in his life this man of God experienced the joy of knowing that he was secure in his eternal salvation.

Did he sin? Yes.

Did his sin prove he wasn't born again? Of course not! But it did show him that this part of his life needed careful attention.

Did his sin prove that he wasn't truly consecrated to the Lord? Again, no. That man would have given everything he had for Christ at that moment, even his very life. His sin did show that although his heart may be devoted to the Lord, his eyes were not yet separated to Him in every situation, nor was he taking every thought captive to the obedience of Christ (see 2 Corinthians 10:5).

Do you see how quickly we can become mixed up? We tend to confuse the stages of holiness. To clarify, the salvation of your soul is not the same as the consecration of your life, which is not the same as the holiness of your character and conduct. God's separating me to Himself in His heart is not the same as my separating myself to Him in my heart, which is not the same as my separating my habits and lifestyle to Him.

The more clearly you understand these three different types of holiness, the easier it will become to make sense of your spiritual life. How then would you answer these questions?

1. Can you be a saint and yet still act unsaintly?
2. Can you be truly born again and yet not be consecrated to the Lord?
3. Can you be consecrated to the Lord and yet still have parts of your life which can be characterized as unholy?
4. Can parts of your character and conduct be truly holy in the eyes of God and man while, at the same time, other areas of your character and conduct are truly unholy?
5. Can you come to know Jesus Christ as your personal Savior and years later experience a crisis of consecration where you genuinely dedicate yourself to Him and then serve Him in obedience?
6. Can you be a born-again Christian, having dedicated yourself to the Lord at church camp when you were fourteen, attend

church semiregularly as an adult, sing in the choir, seldom have meaningful personal devotions, rarely pray except at meals and church functions, read your Bible twice a week, watch TV more than twenty hours a week, rent numerous R-rated movies, not really grow spiritually, attend a revival conference at your church and genuinely repent of your lack of holiness in character and conduct, die on the way home, and still go to heaven?

Personal holiness is one of the simplest yet most challenging truths in all of the Bible, and most believers understandably lose their sense of balance in this area. Allow me to address a few of the more common misconceptions regarding holiness. See if you can identify with any of them or know of family or friends who are currently trapped in these holiness dead ends.

"If I am truly born again, I will automatically live a holy life."
What bondage this notion places over God's people! The thought that salvation equals holiness is usually caused by a misunderstanding of 2 Corinthians 5:17, "Therefore, if anyone is in Christ, he is a new creation; old things have passed away; behold, all things have become new."

Salvation grants us eternal life and the gift of the Holy Spirit, but it does not grant us sinless perfection. The New Testament is filled with letters written to Christians who were living like non-Christians. Again and again, the apostle Paul confronts their behavior and tells them to change it—but by *obeying* Christ, not *believing* in Him anew. If you want ample proof that born-again men and women can and do sin, just read 1 Corinthians.

"All of us are sinners and sin all the time, so no one can ever truly be holy."

It is the will of God that you and I be holy in all our ways. Is that possible for us mere humans? Consider these words of Paul and Peter:

> Let everyone who names the name of Christ depart from iniquity. (2 Timothy 2:19)

> But as He who called you is holy, you also be holy in all your conduct. (1 Peter 1:15)

Can you ever know a period in your life when you are holy in all your conduct? Of course! That's the point. Progressive holiness means that, by God's grace, you will find there are longer and longer time periods between your sins.

"I will finally be made holy when I have a crisis holiness experience."

There are many different names for this kind of "crisis experience," depending upon your tradition of worship. For many, this crisis experience is actually the act of dedicating oneself to live for Christ—the second stage of holiness. Although presenting yourself to the Lord should dramatically influence your life, it will not instantly erase all struggle with sin. Even Peter, who was incredibly and honestly consecrated to Christ in the Upper Room, later denied Him.

Others link a baptism of the Holy Spirit, or becoming "Spirit-filled," with the eradication of all sin. While no one would ever deny that the Holy Spirit holds a central place in any discussion regarding holiness, can such an event eradicate sin in your life? Once again the New Testament provides a ready answer. Of all New Testament churches, the church of Corinth undeniably overflowed with individuals who were baptized, filled, and gifted by the Spirit. Yet of all the New Testament churches, the Corinthians were clearly not among the most experientially holy.

The truth? While genuine crisis experiences can radically affect one's commitment to holiness, they do not bring us to a point of enduring holiness. That's perhaps the reason Paul commanded us to keep on being filled with the Spirit in order not to fulfill the lusts of the flesh (see Ephesians 5:18).

HOW SHOULD I THINK OF HOLINESS IN MY LIFE TODAY?

Before seeking to answer that profound and strategic question, let me ask you a preliminary question. How holy would you say that you are in this season of your life? Be as honest as you can and select the answer that you feel best describes your current state of personal holiness:

❑ Don't ask. I haven't made much progress toward holiness yet.

❑ I'm kind of average, like most of the church people I know.

❑ Holiness has become more important to me, and I've made some changes.

❑ I'm a long way from being holy, but my character and conduct are more Christlike than they were a couple of years ago.

❏   Personal holiness is extremely important to me. I'm actively
    pursuing the Lord and have cleansed whole areas of my life.

I don't believe the Lord intends for us to be mystified or bewil-
dered regarding holiness or to become frustrated in our attempts to
become more like Him. So let's see if we can't make the conceptual
more concrete and the profound more practical.

PART TWO

Victory over Temptation

Chapter 5

How to Grow
in Holiness

*I have conquered an empire,
but I have not been able to conquer myself.*

PETER THE GREAT

ird up your loins, as Paul might say. Or in modern terms,
roll up your sleeves. Because this chapter is a hands-on,
practical approach to the question of what you must do to
grow in holiness. No deep theology or high-falutin' philosophy in
this chapter—just straightforward, commonsense communication
about daily living in holiness.

By this time, I hope that holiness has been repositioned in your
heart and that you are ready to learn how to actually grow as someone separated to the Lord. Hold in your mind the key principle of
2 Corinthians 7:1, that God calls you to bring to full completion
your personal holiness.

The Two Halves of Holiness

Before you can truly pursue personal holiness, you must understand the principal methods for actually growing in holiness. It doesn't come naturally. In fact, the Bible reveals that *unholiness* comes naturally! Therefore, prepare yourself. Take purposeful steps in the right direction, or you might end up heading the wrong way on a one-way street.

Embedded in 2 Timothy 2:19–22 lie two halves of holiness:

"Let everyone who names the name of Christ depart from iniquity." But in a great house there are not only vessels of gold and silver, but also of wood and clay, some for honor and some for dishonor. Therefore if anyone cleanses himself from the latter, he will be a vessel for honor, sanctified [holy], and useful for the Master, prepared for every good work. Flee also youthful lusts; but pursue righteousness, faith, love, peace with those who call on the Lord out of a pure heart.

Four key actions in this passage reveal what the Lord requires from all who would be people of honor, holy and prepared for every good work:

1. "Depart from iniquity" (i.e., leave sin)
2. "Cleanse himself" (leave your old, unholy ways)
3. "Flee also youthful lusts" (leave your selfish desires)
4. "Pursue righteousness" (chase after holiness)

The first half of holiness focuses on leaving something behind—departing from iniquity, cleansing yourself from sin, and fleeing lusts. The second half of holiness focuses on chasing after something—pursuing righteousness.

Picture yourself standing on the timeline of your life. Look back over your shoulder to those areas which are unholy in the Lord's eyes. Your mission is to flee and cleanse yourself from these things. That's the first half of holiness. Now look forward in time to Jesus Christ standing at the end of your life, beckoning you to become as He is in character and conduct. Don't wait! Begin to pursue righteousness *now*—with His help. That's the second half of holiness.

Hebrews 12:1–2 reveals these same two halves of holiness:

> Therefore we also, since we are surrounded by so great a cloud of witnesses, let us lay aside every weight, and the sin which so easily ensnares us, and let us run with endurance the race that is set before us, looking unto Jesus, the author and finisher of our faith.

Similarly, Hebrews describes the first half of holiness as laying aside sin and the second half as running with endurance the race to become like Jesus. It's interesting that, in both passages, the author clearly assumes that his readers first must cleanse themselves from present sin and then pursue righteousness. Don't ever allow yourself to believe—even for an instant—that you are an exception to both of these admonitions!

Paul elaborated on the two halves of holiness in a letter to the church at Colosse:

But now you yourselves are to put off all these: anger, wrath, malice, blasphemy, filthy language out of your mouth. Put on tender mercies, kindness, humility, meekness, longsuffering; bearing with another, and forgiving one another. (Colossians 3:8, 12–13)

Notice the order? First "put off," then "put on." Although each of these are separate acts, they are both necessary for you to grow in holiness.

THE STRATEGIC IMPORTANCE OF CLEANSING YOURSELF

Cleansing oneself from all known sin is one of the most difficult things for the believer to do. You may not have thought a great deal about your sin to this point. Dealing with personal sin doesn't seem to be at the top of most Christians' to-do list. That is, until we decide to aggressively pursue holiness—then we have no choice!

All growth in personal holiness is predicated on the cleansing of personal sin. Why? Because your sin is nothing less than personal *unholiness.* Erwin Lutzer wrote, "We must not part with sin, as with a friend, with a purpose to see it again and to have the same familiarity with it as before, or possibly greater.... We must shake our hands of it as Paul did shake the viper off his hand into the fire."

Any pursuit of holiness must begin by handling those areas of your life which you have permitted to remain beyond the will of God. When you move toward holiness, you no longer seek to defend or rationalize your sin; you only want to get it out of your life. *The greater your desire for holiness, the more eager you become to be fully cleansed and have a clean conscience before God.*

Do you know what the Bible calls such a movement toward personal cleansing? The stirrings of revival. Personal revival begins when a born-again believer who has slid backward in the Christian life gets right with the Lord. And when enough Christians in one place get right with God, they stir the embers and eventually fan the flames of a full-blown revival.

But you will never experience any kind of revival or success in the pursuit of righteousness without first asking the Lord to cleanse you from sin. Even people who have devotions on a daily basis may not be walking in holiness. They may worship and praise the Lord but not please Him. The believer must cleanse himself *and* commune with the Lord. One without the other will bring you up short. For example, people who focus on cleansing their sin without daily communing with God often tend to become harsh, judgmental, and legalistic.

Notice the strategic balance of positive holiness and negative holiness in the central passage of Scripture regarding revival (corporate holiness) in 2 Chronicles 7:14:

If My people who are called by My name will humble themselves, and pray and seek My face, and turn from their wicked ways, then I will hear from heaven, and will forgive their sin and heal their land.

Did you see it? "Turn from their wicked ways" occurs *before* revival, not after it! The first step toward holiness is always cleaning up the sin in your life.

One of the most powerful and pervasive lies of the enemy is that you are currently unable to turn from your wicked ways right now, that until God helps you to really desire holiness, you cannot do it—it's just too difficult.

The Alarming Truth About Sin in the Church Today

Earlier, I said that my experience tells me the vast majority of Christians are not actively pursuing personal holiness. Only a small minority of Christians are in any serious way seeking to become holy in all their conduct.

Think about the Christians you know. How many of them are openly seeking to become holy in their character and conduct? Recently, I had the privilege of serving in a missions movement that sends one-year missionaries to the former Soviet Union. For the most part, these were the cream of the crop among the laypeople of our best churches. They sensed the Lord's call on their lives and left everything behind to serve the Lord.

The leadership of this grand movement asked if I would minister to each group before they departed on assignment. So at each of twelve training sessions, I led these missionary recruits (average age was thirty-five to forty-five) who had been Christians for most of their lives (twenty-five to thirty years) through a session of personal cleansing of sin.

After teaching the biblical principles of cleansing, I had the missionaries pray and ask the Lord to reveal all the unconfessed sin that grieved Him and lay between Him and each individual. They then wrote down all the specifics the Lord revealed to them during those convicting moments—broken relationships, immorality, lying, stealing, rebellion to authority, or anything else. Then I asked them to raise their hands if the Lord had brought at least three or four significant sins to mind. More than 95 percent of this dedicated group raised their hands!

Then I challenged them to do whatever it would take to have a clean conscience before they were officially commissioned in three days. When each item had been addressed, they were to write the word *done* next to it, so we could see their progress and pray and encourage them.

> *One of the most powerful lies of the enemy is that holiness is just too difficult.*

After leading this type of group training five or six times over the years with hundreds of adults, I finally asked this question of one group after they had their lives completely cleansed of all known sin: "How many of you would say that this was the very first time in your entire life you experienced a completely clean life before the Lord?" More than 70 percent of these dedicated Christians raised their hands.

Let that soak in for a moment.

Did you think I was exaggerating when I said the vast majority of believers are not walking in holiness? Ninety percent of the cream of the crop confessed to numerous known sins. Seventy percent of departing missionaries said this was the first time in their entire lives they were ever cleansed. If a believer realizes he has three major sins between him and the Lord, would you say he is walking in holiness?

How many are on your list right now?

Obviously, your feelings about sin greatly influence whether you choose to sin. Choose one of the following perspectives that best describes you at this time in your life:

1. I actively pursue personal sin.
2. I don't think much about it; sin just happens.
3. I try to avoid sin most of the time.
4. I feel regret when I sin.
5. I become angry when I sin.
6. I become deeply grieved when I sin.
7. I hate and detest sin and turn from it.

Get in touch now with how the Lord feels about sin. If you are not where you should be, ask the Lord to change your mind and mold your emotions to match His heart's response to your sin.

WHERE DO YOU STAND ON YOUR SIN?

After working with many Christians in this area, I've observed five distinct seasons the normal Christian progresses through on the way to significant holiness through personal cleansing. Identify which of these best describes where you are—and what needs to happen next.

1. Rejection of Cleansing Due to Hardness of Heart

During this season of the Christian life, the believer hardens his heart against the Lord due to a desire to continue in sin. The believer doesn't have a devotional life, doesn't feel close to the Lord, feels defeated, and is in bondage to at least one major sin.

2. Sporadic Cleansings Due to Powerful External Influences

During this season of the Christian life, the believer does respond to the convicting work of the Holy Spirit in his life, but never purposefully. In other words, some painful experience or some powerful preacher touches his heart, and the Christian responds with genuine repentance but does not change his life to any lasting degree.

3. Initial Deep Cleansing and Intense Desire for the Lord

During this season of the Christian life, the believer has been growing spiritually. He has been engaging in daily devotions, serving the Lord with more fulfillment and fruitfulness, and enjoying actual communion with Christ from time to time. Due to the unexpected pleasure and joy of his relationship with Jesus, the believer now desperately desires more of the Lord and asks the Lord to show him the path to know Him more deeply.

Because the believer has fulfilled all four conditions for revival—humbled himself, prayed, sought the Lord, and turned from long-standing sins—the Lord responds at a deeper level than the believer has ever experienced. During this initial deep cleansing, the believer will beg the Lord to reveal every sin that blocks a deeper walk with Him. It's not uncommon in this stage for the believer to make a long list of specific sins that have never been dealt with properly. This will be the first time in the believer's life in which the Lord opens his eyes to the breadth and depth of his personal sin. A deeper understanding of grace and humility always accompanies this third level.

4. Repeated Deep Cleansings and a Hunger for Holiness

After the initial deep cleansing, the believer may think that his heart is now fully cleansed before the Lord. But as the growing Christian continues to seek the Lord, the Lord will put in his heart the desire to be more and more Christlike. The believer will plead with the

Lord to permit him to serve Christ more and to enjoy a more intimate walk with Him. The hindrance to answering this request lies directly in the more entrenched sins in the life of the believer. During this season, the Lord will expose these deeper levels of sin so the believer may truly cleanse himself.

And so the cleansing of the believer moves from the external to the internal to the eternal. First, there is the *cleansing of conduct,* in which we ask the Lord to cleanse us of what we do. Second is the *cleansing of character,* in which we cleanse ourselves of who we are. Third is the *cleansing of the core,* in which we cleanse ourselves of why we do what we do.

These cleansings may require anywhere from a couple of months to a decade, depending on the believer's response and the depth of his sin. The deeper the cleansing, the more painful and difficult our sins are to deal with fully. Holiness has a tremendous price tag, and when you meet a truly holy individual you can be sure his life has passed through numerous fires of purification.

Once you have passed into the character cleansing, others will notice in you a kinder, gentler, more loving, and more joyful countenance. But the core cleansing deals with true motives. Root issues such as selfish ambition, envy, jealousy, and desire for self-glorification surface and must be rooted out by the Lord's deep work in the life and heart and soul of the believer.

5. Regular Cleansing and a Deepening Relationship with the Lord

During this season, the believer has been humbled deeply and has learned the joy of walking ever deeper with the Lord. Because the believer's heart has been so tenderized, he now becomes so utterly sensitive to sin that he quickly cleanses himself through the principles outlined in 1 John (listed below). He also becomes aware of the person and presence of the Holy Spirit in a deeper way than ever before.

The believer grows in his intimate relationship with the Holy Spirit. He learns of His gentle nature, His loyalty, kindness, compassions, and ever-enduring tenderness. This relationship with the Spirit is treasured greatly, and the believer learns more and more what grieves and quenches the Spirit.

During this season, the believer keeps close accounts with the Lord and confesses and makes restoration moment by moment, so larger and deeper cleansings are no longer necessary. For a period, it may appear that the cleansings will never end, but at last they do. How free and joyful is the believer who knows the freedom of walking in purity of body, soul, and spirit.

TEN STEPS TO DEEP CLEANSING

The greatest hindrance to holiness isn't primarily a problem of motivation, but one of accumulation. Believers often experience frustration and defeat in their spiritual lives as the direct result of a grimy buildup of unconfessed sins.

You can prepare yourself for a ten-step deep cleansing by meditating on 1 John 1:9: "If we confess our sins, He is faithful and just to forgive us our sins and to cleanse us from all unrighteousness." Confession is the key ingredient here. Our confession means we *agree with God*—we acknowledge having sinned against Him.

Whatever deep and difficult problems may have plagued you for years, you cannot fathom now the utter freedom and sense of joy you will experience at the end of this process:

1. *Find a quiet place to sit alone* for at least one hour with several sheets of paper, a pen, and your favorite Bible.

2. *Quiet your heart before the Lord* by sitting still, closing your eyes, and preparing to seek the Lord. Put all distractions and worries out of your mind. Don't be frustrated; this may take a few moments.

3. *Pray to the Lord and thank Him* for bringing you to this place, where you desire to be cleansed before Him. Ask Him to give you courage and grace as you humble yourself. Commit to the Lord that you will stay in the process until He reveals that you are fully cleansed, regardless of the cost.

4. *Ask the Holy Spirit, "Please reveal to me the specific sins in my life,* even the ones I may have forgotten, which lie between You and me. In Jesus' name, amen."

5. *List everything the Holy Spirit reveals to you.* Don't hesitate, and don't skip any of the harder ones. When you can't think of any more, pray a second time, "Holy Spirit, I desire to confess all sins between You and me. Please reveal any additional sins. Give me Your courage and grace." After you have listed everything, sit quietly for five minutes—time yourself—and you may receive a couple more. When the list is completed, number what's on the list in the order of how difficult they will be for you to confess and make restoration, number one being the hardest.

6. *Confess your sins* one at a time before the Lord. Begin with the hardest first, using words like these: "Lord, I hereby confess to You that I have committed the sin of _____. Please forgive me for this sin and thoroughly cleanse me from it." Go through your list one by one until you are finished.

7. *Anticipate the personal struggle you will face.* Don't be alarmed at your strong desire to flee; everyone feels the same way! Just proceed with your commitment. And give yourself a maximum of three days to make right every single item on your list.

8. *Make restoration wherever necessary and expect to have to humble yourself to at least one other person* in the process of restoration. Take the hardest first and deal with it in person. If that's not possible, use the telephone. If that's not possible, write a letter. Sometimes you will have to return to a store and pay for items you stole or confess to a teacher that you cheated on an exam. Always take the high road and do more than what would be expected of you.

9. *Write DONE! across your sheet* after you have confessed, made restoration, forgiven, and received God's cleansing for each sin. When every item is completed, burn your sheet as an act of assurance of the Lord's total and complete forgiveness. Then realize that any negative thoughts about what you've done are not from God, and never allow the accuser to attack you on these issues again. For tough cases, just pray these words out loud: "Lord, I have confessed this sin of _____ and I know You have forgiven me. I stand in Your forgiveness and cleansing."

10. *Thank the Lord* when you have completed your list. Praise Him for His forgiveness and thank Him for His cleansing. And if you would like to encourage one other person with your victory, send me a simple handwritten card, in care of my publisher, with your name on it and the word *DONE!* That's all—just to encourage me that people like you are pursuing righteousness with their whole heart.

Rinse and Repeat for Regular Cleansing

Once this ten-step cleansing is completed, you may be surprised to find the Lord leading you to repeat this process two or three times in the weeks and months ahead. As you grow closer to Him, He may reveal other sins you have forgotten from earlier in your life. Don't be surprised. Instead, anticipate it. Take courage, prepare yourself, and repeat the ten steps to personal cleansing.

This cleansing cycle is also preventative and will soon eliminate the need for *major* cleansings. Among those who walk with God, this is often called "keeping short accounts with the Lord," which means that we minimize the time between our commission and confession of a sin. Obviously, none of us desires to sin; but until we enter heaven's gates, we will.

So consider undergoing cleansing on a regular basis, keeping in mind some different "rinse cycles" that will keep you growing closer to Him.

Moment-to-Moment Cycle

Any time you commit a sin, whether of commission or omission, instantly confess it to the Lord and make any necessary restitution. The more you do this, the more powerful the process will become as a preventative tool. And it will certainly build discipline!

Daily Cycle

When you hold your personal devotions, always set aside a specific portion of your prayer time during which you quietly wait on the

Lord and ask Him if there were any issues from the previous day that need confession.

Weekly Cycle

Throughout church history, the Sabbath and/or Sunday have been used for deeper self-examination and confession. Perhaps the last hour of Sunday night would be a valuable time to get alone and review the past—and upcoming—week, but from the Lord's perspective instead of yours. You may be surprised how this will surface areas needing your attention and confession.

Monthly Cycle

On the first day of each month, I read through my journal to glean life lessons the Lord is currently trying to teach me. This morning I began to see more clearly how a certain one of my deeply entrenched values did not reflect the perfect will of God. Now I can address this issue.

Yearly Cycle

Many Christian leaders I know invest considerable time between Christmas and New Year's Eve each year reading through their personal and prayer journals to examine what the hand of the Lord has been doing in their lives during the past year. This perspective can be entirely fresh and invigorating. As you read through the last year of your life, areas which were confessed and forsaken earlier in the year no longer surface later in the year. Areas which were still foggy early in the year can now be seen quite clearly. Few things can beat twelve months of hindsight!

Chapter 6

The Truth About Temptation

No man knows how bad he is until he has tried to be good.
There is a silly idea about that good people
don't know what temptation means.

C. S. LEWIS

*I*f you could destroy your enemy's ability to bring temptation into your life, he would be instantly powerless.

Think about how temptation actually works in your life. How does a person like you, who is born again and loves the Lord, ever move from being holy to unholy? What is the primary path by which a believer moves from obedience to disobedience, from righteousness to unrighteousness?

The same strategy of temptation is unleashed millions of times every day on the unsuspecting masses. Is this strategy effective? Well, for the vast majority, it's all that's ever needed. Even you, the last time you fell into sin, were actually maneuvered by the same hands of temptation that have always pushed or pulled you in the past.

Another word to describe a temptation is *incentive*. An incentive is something that motivates or incites a person to do something. In the business world, incentives are widely used. For instance, when you walk into a store where two competing soft drinks are on sale, if one advertises *Buy one and get one free!* what are you motivated (or tempted) to do? As a parent, you may often use some kind of incentive to encourage your children to keep their rooms clean or strive for good grades.

Are incentives wrong? Not if they encourage correct behavior. Indeed, as you read through the Bible, you can't miss the fact that God Himself frequently uses incentives to motivate His followers.

However, incentives can be used for evil ends as well, at which point they become temptations. With such understanding of this process comes the power to resist temptation and break any authority it might have over you. So let's get started.

THE KEY PASSAGE ABOUT TEMPTATION

When you want to grasp a truth of God's Word, always begin by searching the Bible for the key passage that contains the most important truth about that topic. Then mine that passage for its secrets.

On the subject of temptation, the key biblical passage is 1 Corinthians 10:12–13. Read it carefully before moving on to the seven statements of truth about temptation, which follow:

> Therefore let him who thinks he stands take heed lest he fall. No temptation has overtaken you except such as is common to man; but God is faithful, who will not allow you to be tempted beyond what you are able, but with the

temptation will also make the way of escape, that you may be able to bear it.

1. Temptation Is the Primary Reason You Desire to Sin

The linkage is unmistakable—the fall into sin is always preceded by the temptation, which has "overtaken you."

When you open to the very first pages of the Bible, what do you find Satan doing? Tempting Adam and Eve to disobey God's command not to eat from the tree of the knowledge of good and evil. Notice the subtle temptations, or incentives, Satan used on Eve:

"You will not surely die." Satan tempted Eve to doubt the clear warning of God. You see, temptation must deal with known truth that is in opposition to the sin, or the sin may not be committed. If Eve hadn't fallen to this temptation to doubt, she might never have given in. *Temptations always minimize the real dangers and maximize the imagined benefits.*

"Your eyes will be opened." Satan subtly implied that Eve's eyes must have been closed—and who made her eyes "not opened" in the first place? What a subtle attack on the character of the Lord, who must have purposely kept them blinded! *Temptations always breed doubt about the word and character of God.*

"You will be like God." Satan incited Eve's imagination with the thought of becoming like God. The temptation made an incredible leap at this point, but it went right by her. At that very moment, Adam and Eve were already more like

God than any living being anywhere in the universe! Adam and Eve were supernaturally created by God in His very image and likeness. But by eating of the tree they chose to become as unlike God as possible. The way Satan proposed they would become like God was to do the exact opposite of what God had told them! *Every single temptation is rooted in at least one massive lie, which is promoted as the answer for what the person is looking for.*

"You will [know] good and evil." Satan knows how tempting forbidden knowledge is to the human. How incredibly deceitful is this temptation! Adam and Eve already knew the fullness of good knowledge—they were in the Garden of Eden, walking with the Almighty! Why would they ever desire to know evil? Here the tempter uses desire, or lust, for something expressly outside the boundaries created for man. Man wasn't created to break through the safety fence separating him from good and evil. By choosing to know that which the Lord purposefully chose to withhold, Adam and Eve fell into the same sin of Satan himself, the desire to independently rule and overthrow the sovereign limitations that God set. *Temptation always incites lust to know and experience evil, which is forbidden by God, in the false pursuit of that which is good.*

Without any temptation or motivation, why would Adam or Eve ever have considered disobeying the Lord? Do you see the critical role of temptation in life? Without it, what could be the motivation for choosing to sin?

Likewise, consider what Satan did in seeking to defeat Jesus—
he offered three powerful temptations. Note how Jesus rebuked
Satan and revealed the very nature of his attack: "You shall not *tempt*
the Lord your God."

Satan will tempt you throughout your entire life. Whatever sin
you have committed was preceded by a temptation, which you
believed and then acted upon by disobeying God and willfully sinning.

2. *Temptations Are Particularly Dangerous When You Think You Can't Fall*

First Corinthians 10:12 begins with a strong warning about temptations: "Therefore let him who thinks he stands take heed lest he
fall." Perhaps this warning is placed first because it reveals the exact
opposite of what a person would normally think about temptation.
Which is better, to think you can't fall into sin or to know you can?

The best answer is found in Proverbs 16:18: "Pride goes before
destruction, and a haughty spirit before a fall." When you think you
can't fall, pride reigns. When pride reigns, destruction will soon follow. Whenever you spot arrogance, whether blatant or carefully
hidden, you can be sure that a fall is already imminent.

What then is the correct attitude and action in the face of temptation, which leads us to victory and not destruction, to a position
of standing rather than falling? These verses reveal the answer—
watchfulness, prayer, and active dependence upon the Lord:

> "Watch and pray, lest you enter into temptation. The spirit
> indeed is willing, but the flesh is weak." (Matthew 26:41)

When He came to the place, He said to them, "Pray that you may not enter into temptation." (Luke 22:40)

Then the Lord knows how to deliver the godly out of temptations. (2 Peter 2:9)

Our focus must always be upon our weakness and upon His strength. As Martin Luther said, "My temptations have been my 'Masters in Divinity.'" Pray daily that the Lord would keep you from temptation, but when it comes, that He would strengthen you in and through it.

3. Temptations Seek to Overtake You

Temptations aren't inactive but active. Temptations don't flee from you, they seek to overtake you, as Paul said in 1 Corinthians 10:13. Even in the most spiritual of activities, temptation can step forward and grab you with power and persistence.

Paul teaches that temptations have an almost independent reality. They come and overtake. They seize. They assail. They grasp. They attempt to hold us down until we finally sin. You'll notice that when you have given in to temptation it no longer exists. Temptations only exist on the "before" side of sin! Before every sin lies its temptation. If you defeat the temptation, you will not commit the sin!

4. Temptations Are Never Unique but Always Common to Everyone

If you have sinned repeatedly in a given area, you may conclude that your temptations aren't of "normal" size and strength, but are unique and irresistible. But the Bible tells us, "No temptation has overtaken you except such as is common to man" (1 Corinthians 10:13).

Now you must also understand that, although every temptation is common, each of us is very different. For instance, one may be tempted in the area of gluttony, another in pornography, another in gossip, and another in anger. Let's say that you and your friend are grocery shopping together. You are tempted in the area of gluttony, so you struggle in the dessert aisle, while your friend faces a different temptation and struggles at the magazine rack. Does that mean you also struggle at the magazine rack? Probably not.

Different temptations attack different people. I also face temptations that are common; but because I might be weak in a particular area, I might give in to a temptation that wouldn't affect you.

After a men's breakfast meeting at which I had spoken on personal holiness, I was approached by a young man who was obviously under conviction. He shared that he longed for major changes in his life but was having great difficulty. He was living with a woman and had lived with numerous women during the past ten years. When I asked why he didn't just stop this immoral and ungodly lifestyle, he said he was powerless in the face of his sexual temptations.

Every temptation is common; each of us is very different.

I said, "Your sex drive must be really strong!"

He said, "Yeah…well, I'm glad you understand. My sex drive is so powerful that my temptations are just huge."

I nodded. "Probably many times larger than the normal man's."

He blushed sheepishly. Finally he had found someone who understood that his sin wasn't really *his* fault—it was those giant temptations that attacked him.

I asked him if it would make any difference if those giant temptations were brought down to normal size. "Wow!" he exclaimed. "I'd give anything to have normal temptations. Why, I'd finally be able to say no and stop."

Then I turned around and scanned the room that was quickly emptying as the men left for work. "So if your temptations were just like Chuck's or Bob's, what would you do?"

"What do you mean, what would I do? About what?"

"About your sinful lifestyle. Would you then obey the Lord and depart from your immoral ways? Only, of course, if your sexual temptations were brought way down to 'normal' size?"

That sounded good to him, and he nodded with nearly carefree abandon. No one could fix his problem, so why worry?

Then I asked him to read 1 Corinthians 10:13 out loud.

"No temptation has overtaken you except such as is common to man."

What a shock to discover that his temptations were nothing more than the garden-variety temptations growing in every man's life. I pointed to another man still lingering in the room and said, "He has the exact same temptation as you do—only he said no and you said yes."

In the next few moments, this young man wrestled against the tragic lie he had believed. That lie had buried him under the heavy load of massive and crippling self-deception. And when that lie was brought directly into the light of the Bible, it fell powerless at his feet. With tears in his eyes, he said, "I'm going to break free today. I'm saying no to my sexual temptations. I'm leaving here...and walking in holiness."

Truth always sets us free; lies always hold us in bondage. If you are in bondage to a sin, it's simply because you believe a lie.

Regardless of what you may have thought about the temptations you face, the Bible teaches that they are absolutely no different from the ones faced by all your neighbors. Think about the lies we tell ourselves:

"It was just too strong. I couldn't help myself!"
"This kind of thing runs in my family."
"I've always done it—it's too late to stop now."
"The devil made me do it."
"I don't worry about temptation; I'm too strong."
"It's not my fault; I was tempted beyond my ability."
"I prayed about the temptation but couldn't stop."
"Lay off—no one's perfect."

But if all temptations are normal and therefore totally resistible, how then can we explain how we feel when those common temptations assail us? Perhaps a little dog might hold the secret to the answer.

Remember the wizard who ruled in the land of Oz? Everyone was fearful to the point of trembling about the strength and power of the wizard, until a scruffy little dog pulled back the sacred curtain! There Dorothy and her friends saw an old, weak little man disguising his voice and surrounding himself with special effects. Do you remember what happened next as they recognized the truth about this "powerful wizard"? The truth set them free.

Pull back the curtain on your temptation and you'll find two things. First, your temptation is the common type growing wild across the human landscape. Second, your temptation is full of hot air and will always disappear into thin air when you simply say no.

5. Temptations Aren't Allowed to Exceed Your Ability to Resist

The times you may think the Lord isn't around certainly would include those times you are tempted to sin. But the Bible reveals that the Lord is intimately involved in every temptation, not by sending it but by making sure you can endure it without giving in to sin. First Corinthians 10:13 continues, "But God is faithful, who will not allow you to be tempted beyond what you are able."

These words from Paul provide wonderful encouragement and guaranteed hope in the face of temptation. You can withstand every temptation—helped by none other than the Lord God of the universe.

Make sure you wrap your mind around this truth. Instead of avoiding you when you are tempted, the Lord approaches you to protect and aid you. He's right there at your side, right there in the battle. Imagine that! Just think of what that means about how intimately the Lord is committed to you and your victory over temptation! Never again believe the lie that the Lord becomes angry or distant when you are in the middle of the temptation; because the truth is that the Lord becomes extremely involved at the very point of temptation. He draws a bold line in the sand and commands that the temptation can go this far, but no farther.

One afternoon while writing this chapter, I took a break and walked around the neighborhood with my wife, Darlene Marie. As we walked, we passed a massive oak tree towering far above our heads. We marveled at the strength and majesty of this tree and how it had withstood decades of storms and winds. I asked Darlene if she thought there could ever be a storm fierce enough to blow it over. She nodded, thinking of news footage of incredibly powerful tornadoes destroying everything in their path.

But will there ever be a "temptation tornado" that can destroy you and crush your strongest commitment to a life of holiness? Never. The Lord protects us and limits the power of every temptation. The Lord graciously limits Satan's freedom in pushing us over the edge.

> *The Lord graciously limits Satan's freedom in pushing us over the edge.*

But what happens when we are repeatedly unfaithful, when we choose to sin in the face of a temptation over and over and over again? Obviously, the Lord must have a limit to His faithfulness depending upon how faithful we are to Him, right? Check out 2 Timothy 2:13 for the answer: "If we are faithless, He remains faithful; He cannot deny Himself."

The truth is that the Lord God will never leave you or forsake you in the face of a temptation. He will always—in every circumstance and at every time—sovereignly limit your temptations so they never exceed your ability to say no. No wonder God says to be holy in all your conduct; He provides everything you need, but limits everything you don't.

A few implications surface immediately from this truth.

God limits the temptations I face according to my abilities, not someone else's.

The Lord has His full attention focused on you and your ability. That means that if you and your friends faced a large and unexpected temptation together, the Lord would limit that particular temptation differently for each individual. The same temptation is limited by the Lord according to the varying abilities of the individuals.

God limits the temptations but doesn't necessarily increase our strength.

Before you is a massive barbell with five hundred pounds of weights. The Lord instructs you to lift the barbell. You bend your knees and call upon everything within you but you cannot budge it. What does the Lord do to help, give you massive muscles? No. The Bible doesn't teach that "God is faithful, who will increase your abilities so you will be able to withstand the temptation."

Instead, God enables you to obey Him by taking weights off the barbell until He knows you can lift it. Therefore, never expect the Lord to miraculously strengthen you, but rather expect Him to miraculously limit the temptation's weight.

God limits temptation according to your circumstances.

Your ability to withstand a temptation is not only different from everyone else's, but also changes according to what is happening in your life. Let's say someone close to you died, you've experienced a major business failure, and you've been sick for an extended time. Would you say that your ability to withstand a specific temptation would be as strong as usual? Certainly not.

I don't know how you feel about the Lord as you understand His incredible faithfulness to you, but His compassion and mercy in protecting me literally overwhelm me. No wonder the Lord can command us to be holy in all our conduct. He makes sure that we can!

6. *Temptations Are Always Accompanied by the Lord's Way of Escape*
Of all the remarkable revelations in these two verses, none is more striking than this provision by God: "But God is faithful, who will not allow you to be tempted beyond what you are able, but with the temptation *will also make the way of escape.*"

God's first provision in the face of temptation is a limitation: He will not allow you to be tempted beyond what you are able. God's second provision in the face of temptation is a provision: He will provide the way of escape.

And a new way of escape is constructed by God with each temptation you face. Previous escape routes that worked in another place might not be of any use to you when you are backed to the edge of a cliff. Because every temptation is different, the escape route must also be different. And God doesn't *find* a way of escape for you; He *makes* a way of escape. When a temptation seeks to overtake you, God sovereignly and uniquely invents and then constructs your safe delivery route out of that temptation.

The more the truth about your temptations becomes clear in your heart and mind, the more His command to "be holy in all your conduct" looks absolutely realistic.

7. *Temptations Cannot Extend Beyond What You Can Bear*

This final principle demonstrates the Lord's heart in His involvement in your temptation. Because He seeks a holy church, He provides for holiness in every situation imaginable: "But God is faithful, who will not allow you to be tempted beyond what you are able, but with the temptation will also make the way of escape, *that you may be able to bear it.*"

The greatest lie about your temptations is, "I can't say no to this temptation no matter how hard I try." Now you know that couldn't be true, or the Lord God is utterly faithless. Never again succumb to this defeating lie, because the moment you entertain it—even for a split second—you've already started down the slippery slide toward sin.

Saying no will not always be easy, but it will always be possible.

However, the Lord may not always reveal the way of escape quickly. In most cases, the way of escape is right before you. Other times, however, the way of escape can require your resisting to the point of physical death.

The ultimate truth is that it is important to stand strong against the temptation to sin even if it may cost you your life. The way of escape for a host of martyred believers has been to stand immovable in the face of the most threatening temptation, even to the point of death.

Although many have paid with their lives, others who knew Christ and His call upon their lives ran into the darkness, denying the Lord who redeemed them in order to save their lives. The lie they listened to and embraced? "I can't do this; this is too hard."

Friend, even death is not too hard, because the Lord will never permit any temptation which will exceed your ability to endure without sin. Those who ran into the darkness ran only because they believed the lie. As long as you are being tempted, you are always able to resist, remaining holy in all your conduct.

THE TRUTH ABOUT TEMPTATION

Two weeks after teaching a group of men this truth about temptation, I bumped into one of them in a local store. You should have heard him go on and on about what the Lord had done in his life during the past two weeks.

He said, "I couldn't believe how deceived I have been all my life about my temptations! I saw them as these towering giants that I was powerless against. After a while, I gave up trying to fight because I thought I couldn't experience victory anyway. Then I learned the truth, and now I know that God stops my temptations dead in their tracks before they can overwhelm me. Now I know that God isn't mad at me when I'm tempted, and I shouldn't hide from Him. He's my true deliverer, providing the way of escape every time. What a God we have!"

The next time you feel like you're beginning to weaken in the face of temptation's lie, speak these words of powerful truth, and you'll be amazed at how the temptations flee into the darkness— right where they came from, and right where they belong. The truth will always set you free!

I realize I am in the middle of a temptation to sin.
I hereby commit to the Lord to depend
upon the Holy Spirit and not sin.
I know the Lord is limiting this temptation,
and it can't be too hard for me.
I know the Lord is making the way
out of this temptation for me.
I am able to bear this temptation until it is over.
I choose to obey the Lord's command
to be "holy in all my conduct."
Thank You, Lord, for Your faithfulness to me!

Chapter 7

Anti-Temptation
Tools for Victory

The holy man is not one who cannot sin.
A holy man is one who will not sin.

A. W. TOZER

lthough the Lord limits your temptation and makes the way of escape, you still must face and overcome your own temptations. You must fight your own battles through to victory. The Bible is very clear that *we* wrestle against darkness and must put on the whole armor of God to withstand evil (see Ephesians 6:12–13).

Holiness lies on the other side of victory over temptation! Let us equip ourselves with powerful tools we can use to defeat temptations. First, you must know how temptations work against you uniquely and then know exactly what to do to enjoy true victory, one battle at a time. I pray that, when you complete this book, you will never again look at your temptations as you do now and that you'll defeat them decisively as you gain skill in using these weapons.

YOUR TEMPTABILITY QUOTIENT

Do you have any idea how vulnerable to attack you are at any given moment? Temptations are carefully timed. They are carefully aimed. Starting in the Garden of Eden, Satan's temptations have succeeded in pulling down even the mightiest men and women by assailing them at their *point* of weakness and at their *moment* of weakness.

Read accounts of individuals in the Bible and you'll see the trend clearly. Temptations attack where and when the believer is weakest and least expecting an assault. Satan tempted Jesus after forty days in the wilderness without food, a moment of physical weakness and isolation. When are you weakest and most vulnerable to temptation?

The "temptability quotient" (TQ) is a remarkable little tool that will take you all of two minutes to use after you've worked through it once. The goal of the TQ is to alert you to how vulnerable you are at a given moment to attacks of temptation. Ten different categories are measured on a scale of 1 to 10. Take a moment to circle the number which best represents your state at this very moment in each category:

Physically Exhausted/Tired	1 2 3 4 5 6 7 8 9 10	Energetic/Strong
Discouraged/Down	1 2 3 4 5 6 7 8 9 10	Encouraged/Up
Bored/Discontent	1 2 3 4 5 6 7 8 9 10	Challenged/Content
Spiritually Depleted/Empty	1 2 3 4 5 6 7 8 9 10	Growing/Full
Distant/Alone	1 2 3 4 5 6 7 8 9 10	Near/Together
Alienated/Cold	1 2 3 4 5 6 7 8 9 10	Relationally Close/Warm
Internally Hopeless/Sad	1 2 3 4 5 6 7 8 9 10	Hopeful/Happy
Insecure/Unsure	1 2 3 4 5 6 7 8 9 10	Secure/Confident
Bitter/Angry	1 2 3 4 5 6 7 8 9 10	Forgiving/Accepting
Wounded/Hurt	1 2 3 4 5 6 7 8 9 10	Appreciated/Loved

After circling where you are right now in these categories, add up the total and you'll find your temptability quotient. Here's how to interpret your score:

90–100 *You're already glorified in heaven!*
80–89 *Very strong, but be alert to subtle pride and arrogance.*
70–79 *Strong, but need to depend more on the Lord.*
60–69 *Adequate, but watch yourself—you're on the border.*
50–59 *Weak—you're emotionally vulnerable.*
40–49 *Danger! Guard yourself—you're floundering.*
30–39 *Extreme danger! Call a Christian friend and yell "Help!"*
20–29 *In the critical ward—probably already fell to major sins.*
10–19 *They're wheeling you into the morgue. Move your toe.*
0–9 *This is a bad dream. Pinch yourself and try again!*

If your score is below seventy, you'd better raise the yellow flag because surf's up and the undertow is much worse than you think. If you fall below sixty, you are definitely in turbulent and troubled waters and heading for a wipeout.

Although Darlene Marie usually knows where I am because we're so close, if I fall below sixty I say, "Sweetheart, I'm feeling really vulnerable. Would you send a few extra prayers up in the next couple of days? And if I'm a little impatient or not too sensitive, remember that it's not you, but me."

If you fall below fifty, you'd better call in some heavy artillery. Call your best friend and encourage him or her to come into your life and lend support. Be certain, however, that you do *not* share these kinds of things with a person of the opposite gender (except your spouse), because you'll be walking directly into a well-worn temptation trap. Never do it. I can't tell you how many friends have shared deep personal issues with a person of the opposite sex, only to pay a horrible price. Protect yourself from further temptation; go to someone of the same sex.

How often should you take your TQ pulse? Probably once a week for twelve weeks in a row. Copy the chart, put it in your Bible, and take the quiz before church on Sunday morning. Select a place and time you can do this every week so it becomes a quick and natural procedure. Record your weekly score on the TQ trend chart below and monitor your progress. This will radically open your eyes.

TQ TREND CHART

Weekly Score	1	2	3	4	5	6	7	8	9	10	11	12
90 – 100												
80 – 89												
70 – 79												
60 – 69												
50 – 59												
40 – 49												
30 – 39												
20 – 29												
10 – 19												
0 – 9												

The TQ trend chart has three categories: the healthy zone, the semidanger zone (the transition zone), and the crisis zone.

All of us move up and down through these zones. For instance, I may score myself one week at fifty-nine, so I will begin watching myself very carefully and pray for the Lord to keep temptation away from me and to strengthen me in the inner man as I yield to His Holy Spirit.

If my score was seventy-six when the week before it was eighty-three, my trend line will raise concern. If the following week my TQ falls below fifty, I'm going to exercise considerable effort before the Lord, alert at least one of my friends, and intensely focus on restoring my life to health and strength.

The value of this trend line is that it gives you a current reading on your spiritual health. If you ever find yourself in the "crisis zone" for two consecutive weeks, be on guard! If you're part of a group working through this study together, consider sharing with each other your TQ score each week. Don't think for a second that your score will be the only one under seventy!

Remember, your score isn't a sign of sin; it's a sign of what's been happening in your life. Don't be discouraged by your score, but instead use it to alert you to vulnerability on your part.

Soon you'll be able to look at your schedule for the coming week and almost predict what you'll be facing. Take measures then to offset the temptations you anticipate. But most important, ask God to lead and strengthen you daily.

UNRAVELING THE BLAME GAME

Every temptation follows a series of steps designed to entice you to sin. But once again, God comes to our rescue by openly teaching us our enemy's strategies. We are not to be ignorant of the devices of our adversary, and indeed God's Word reveals the precise method of attack the enemy employs against us. Get a handle on this strategy and you will be able to anticipate when and where temptations may be lurking in the shadows.

The seven basic stages of temptation are outlined in James 1:13–17. In a moment, we are going to examine each of these seven stages. But first, carefully read the passage from beginning to end:

Let no one say when he is tempted, "I am tempted by God"; for God cannot be tempted by evil, nor does He Himself tempt anyone. But each one is tempted when he is drawn away by his own desires and enticed. Then, when desire has conceived, it gives birth to sin; and sin, when it is full-grown, brings forth death. Do not be deceived, my beloved brethren. Every good gift and every perfect gift is from above, and comes down from the Father of lights, with whom there is no variation or shadow of turning.

James begins his analysis of temptation with a direct attack upon the deepest lie about temptation. After the true consequences of a sin finally hit home, inevitably the person begins looking for someone else to blame. The blame gets passed around until, finally, there is no one left to blame but God.

This is the way it's been from the very beginning, when God said to Adam, "Have you eaten from the tree of which I commanded you that you should not eat?" Adam blamed Eve for his sin. When God said to Eve, "What is this you have done?" Eve blamed her sin on the serpent.

But Adam didn't stop at blaming Eve. He said, "The woman *whom You gave to be with me,* she gave me of the tree, and I ate" (Genesis 3:12). Adam was trying to say, "God, *You* gave me the woman. If You hadn't, then I wouldn't have sinned. You sent the temptation by giving me Eve. Therefore, don't hold me accountable, for I am innocent."

Sound familiar? How about this one? *If God knows everything, then He knew I would sin when this happened. He should have stopped the temptation sooner.* Here's another: *I prayed but God didn't take away the temptation, so it's not my fault.*

Whenever you find yourself thinking, *If God had only...* or *It's not my fault because...,* you are treading on the "blame fault line," which can trigger a massive earthquake in your life. Remember, the Lord never tempts anyone.

James reminds us that instead of darts of destruction, God sends to us "every good gift and every perfect gift." Get this clearly in your mind: God is *never* the author of temptation; God is *always* the author of every good thing in your life.

THE SEVEN STAGES OF EVERY TEMPTATION

Sometimes you stumble upon a gold mine of truth in which, the more you dig, the greater the treasure you discover. James 1:14–15 contains only three dozen words, but they unveil the inner workings of every temptation:

> But each one is tempted when he is drawn away by his own desires and enticed. Then, when desire has conceived, it gives birth to sin; and sin, when it is full-grown, brings forth death.

Here is how James breaks down the seven stages of temptation:

1.	THE LOOK	*"when he is drawn away"*
2.	THE LUST	*"by his own desires"*
3.	THE LURE	*"and enticed"*
4.	THE CONCEPTION	*"when desire has conceived"*
5.	THE BIRTH	*"it gives birth to sin"*
6.	THE GROWTH	*"and sin, when it is full-grown"*
7.	THE DEATH	*"brings forth death"*

STAGE ONE: THE LOOK

This first stage is called "the look" because it's an open door into the land of temptation. James borrows the words *drawn away* from a fishing and hunting context, in which an unsuspecting fish is drawn out of its retreat under a bank or an animal is lured into an area where traps have been set. The picture is of a person being distracted with something that draws his attention away from the task at hand.

Think about being drawn away. This is the subtle if not imperceptible moment in which you slide from a safe position into a risky state corresponding to the earliest stage of temptation. An attractive person of the opposite sex walks past you. A person cuts right in front of you on the way to work. A unique scent calls to mind memories of previous sins. A cashier mistakenly gives you too much change. You overhear a tasty piece of gossip.

Skilled temptation warriors learn to discern almost instantly when they are being drawn away—and instantly draw back! Unless you are drawn *away* from what you are doing, you can't be drawn *into* temptation. If you don't go through that doorway, you cannot be tempted!

The secret to stage one: *Draw back instantly when you sense you're being drawn away!*

STAGE TWO: THE LUST

A lonely housewife cries, "When I get depressed, I can hear the bottle calling to me." A disgruntled worker protests, "My boss is unfair, so I figured I'd get even by stealing from the company." An unhappy man claims, "If my wife were more attentive, I wouldn't have to look for satisfaction elsewhere."

Let's conduct a "temptation check." See if you can put your finger on the major sources of temptation in your own life. Identify:

1. The *person* who tempts you
2. The *situation* in which you are tempted
3. The *activity* that tempts you
4. The *place* where you are tempted
5. The *thought* that most often tempts you

What if all those things that tempt you most often would just disappear? How wonderful life would be! Holiness would be a snap if your sources of temptation disappeared. Right?

Wrong. Try these shocking words on for size: "But each one is tempted when he is drawn away *by his own desires* and enticed." In other words, the only reason a temptation is even tempting is because of our own desires. If you didn't harbor the desire somewhere in your life, that tempting thing, person, or situation wouldn't faze you. Our hidden desires draw us away every time, for without such desires, why on earth would we pursue *anything?*

As I write this, I'm in the middle of a month-long diet with the goal of losing ten pounds. It's three-thirty in the afternoon and hunger is beginning to knock on the walls of my stomach. If my wife were to come downstairs right about now with a little snack of chocolate-chip cookies and some hot coffee, I would be sorely tempted!

But let's say I just finished a huge meal, topped off by a delicious piece of blueberry pie for dessert. A few minutes later Darlene Marie brings me a couple of cookies. Would I be tempted then? No. So what's the difference between the two snack scenarios? My vulnerability to temptation. You see, temptations tempt you because of what's inside of you, not what's outside of you.

When the young man I counseled recently said, "But she tempts me so bad," was that really the truth? No—his lustful heart is the problem, not the woman. Or how about the teenager who told me, "I couldn't help myself; the money lying on the counter was just too tempting"? A covetous heart was the source of his temptation, not a few unguarded bills and coins.

When the Bible says "by his own desire," the word *desire* means anything that attracts you, anything you long for earnestly. Desiring food is good; your need for food and your desire for it is God-given. But if you allow your desire for food to run out of control, you are in danger of commiting the sin of gluttony. God placed all of man's desires within him as a sovereign act of creation. But with each of those desires, God gave man the appropriate means to gratify each of his legitimate desires without sinning.

Temptation always preys upon a God-given desire. It simply tries to distort that desire or push it toward sin in one of two directions—either by pushing the God-given desire past its normal limits into excess, or by pushing the God-given desire to find fulfillment in areas that are "off limits."

Either way, the core of every one of your temptations is in your heart. So every time you feel tempted, you now know what desire is lurking in your heart at that very moment.

The secret to stage two: *Every temptation can only tempt you because of your personal desire.*

Stage Three: The Lure

This third stage is called "the lure" because that's what enticement involves. To entice means to attract artfully, or skillfully, by arousing hope or desire. If you've spent much time fishing, you know the importance of using the right lure—one that moves with the right action through the water and arouses the fish.

Enticement is the stage at which the desire in you grows from a tiny spark to a burning flame. This is the stage at which you really *want* to do something. As your desire increases, you become less aware of everything else in your life, and you become incredibly focused on that one thing. Intense desire blinds us, doesn't it? The most expressive passage about how this happens is found in Proverbs 7:10–22:

> And there a woman met him, with the attire of a harlot, and a crafty heart.... At times she was outside, at times in the open square, lurking at every corner. So she caught him and kissed him; with an impudent face she said to him: "Come, let us take our fill of love until morning; let us delight ourselves with love. For my husband is not at home; he has gone on a long journey...." With her enticing speech she caused him to yield, with her flattering lips she seduced him. Immediately he went after her, as an ox goes to the slaughter.

Another verse, Proverbs 6:25, demonstrates both the internal and external sides of enticement: "Do not lust after her beauty in your heart [your internal enticement], nor let her allure you with her eyelids" [her external enticement].

Stage three occurs as dry wood is thrown (usually by actions of others) onto the smoldering fire of your desire (your heart). The point is to get you focused on just one thing—feeding the flames of desire until you don't care what it costs you to attain the object of your desire.

In an area of temptation where you have sinned very little or not at all, it's very difficult for your desire to grow large enough that you choose to sin in a major way. However, if you have given in to temptation in a specific area many times, when that same temptation pokes its deceitful head above the horizon, your desire can flash so quickly that it may seem like you never passed through the enticement stage. But the fact is that your desire didn't need to be stoked; it was already committed to repeat the sinful patterns you've established.

The good news is that enticement can be stopped. If your temptation is external, run away. If your temptation is internal, guard the self-talk carefully. The quicker you douse the growing flames, the easier it will be to tame and control your desires. When your desires are controlled, the temptation fades.

The secret to stage three: *Quench improper desire by stopping all internal enticements and fleeing all external enticements.*

STAGE FOUR: THE CONCEPTION

Every temptation is instigated with only one goal in mind: to cause you to sin. First the temptation draws you away; then your desire responds; then enticement fans the flames of your desire. Next your desire finally "conceives" and you make the decision to sin. Note carefully the flow of this verse: "But each one is tempted when he is drawn away by his own desires and enticed. Then, *when desire has conceived*, it gives birth to sin."

When does enticement end and conception begin? The moment you decide to fulfill your desire by sinning, enticement sits down, its work finished. Enticement is the powerful link between desire and decision. The flow of enticement drives desire right up that ramp until it overwhlems your decision-making faculties. That's why, when you make the decision to commit the sin, you feel almost relieved or experience some type of emotional release. The pressure falls away, and now it's time to sin.

Here our feelings, thoughts, and choices overlap and influence each other. We move from desire to defending our desire to, finally, deciding we will sin.

THE THREE PHASES OF ENTICEMENT

Desire (feelings) ➜ Defend (thoughts) ➜ Decide (choices)

During the *desire* phase, you experience growing emotional attraction to the temptation and you feel more strongly that you want to respond to it. The desire eventually affects your thoughts, seeking justification or rationalization for giving in to the sin.

During the *defend* phase, you rationalize why committing this sin is really justified. Two defense tactics are always used, the negative and the positive. To commit the sin, you must diminish the reasons not to do it (negative) and emphasize the reasons to do it (positive). Emotions by themselves never have the power to cause the person to sin; the mind and will are always involved and must give their permission and affirmation.

You slowly move the weights on the scale to shift the balance away from reasons not to do something toward reasons to do it. Sometimes you actually throw the reasons not to do something right off the scales, or just stuff them deep within the caverns of your mind.

The most powerful of all reasons to commit a sin comes into play when you take a reason *not* to sin and turn it into a reason *to* sin. It's amazing how creative we can be when our emotions begin pushing us. For instance, a married woman who is tempted to have an affair may start by reasoning, "No, I am married and I made my vows," and then destroy those reasons with memories of all the bad things her husband has done to her. She ends up choosing to sin, reasoning, "He is only getting what he deserves!"

During the *decide* phase, you make your final choice. This is the last phase of the conception stage, when you decide to commit the sin and begin planning when and how you will actually do it.

Now feeling, thinking, and planning all occur within your conscious mind. We're not talking about feelings or thoughts that are subconscious, but conscious and right out in the open. Although you may not have noticed them before, they are the lead actors in every temptation you have ever undergone.

At this point you should be asking yourself, *What am I feeling that I want to do? How long have I been feeling this way?*

Then you need to ask, *What am I thinking? Am I looking for reasons to commit this sin? Am I trying to justify the sin I want to commit?*

Finally you should ask, *What am I planning to do? When and where would I commit this sin? Have I pictured it in my imagination?*

By asking these simple questions, you'll discern where you are within these three early but dangerous phases. So what should you do when you discover where you are?

First of all, realize that you have not yet committed the sin, so it's not too late. Recommit yourself to the truth by affirming out loud such things as:

1. I am committed to live "holy in all my conduct."
2. I submit to the Lord and choose His will for my life.
3. I yield to the Holy Spirit and His work in my life.
4. I deny myself the lusts of the flesh.
5. I realize this is only a common temptation that everyone faces.
6. I believe the Lord is limiting this temptation to what I am able to bear.
7. I believe the Lord is making the way of escape for me right now.
8. I know the Lord is not the cause of this temptation.
9. I know the Lord is the giver of every good and perfect gift.
10. I know the Lord loves me and wants the best for me.
11. I know this sin not only displeases the Lord but will hurt me.
12. I have been drawn away by this temptation.
13. I have felt my desires pulling me toward this temptation.
14. I take every thought captive for Christ and stop all thoughts about this sin.
15. I am fully aware of this temptation and am not deceived.
16. I know this temptation is aimed at my destruction.
17. I hereby choose to turn my back on this temptation.
18. I submit fully to Christ and resist the devil.
19. I present myself and all my members as weapons of righteousness.
20. I thank the Lord for His shed blood and my eternal salvation.

By praying and stating these truths—the truth shall set you free!—you will break the back of the lie. You'll be amazed at how quickly the temptation will flee into the night when you bring out the Light!

The "quick-spit principle" is a humorous but helpful insight taken from a Colorado fishing trip with my son, David. We had a guide who took us to a "hot" trout stream, where he guaranteed we could catch all we wanted. "It's so good that every time you cast with one of my handcrafted lures, you're sure to catch a fish." He was also quick to remind us that this was a catch-and-release stream, so we could use only barbless hooks.

He took us out to his spot, positioned us along the edge of the stream, and directed us to cast the fly in one particular area, letting it drift with the current. I hit the spot dead on and watched the fly drift downstream. Nothing. As I prepared to recast, our guide said, "You just missed him." I repeated the same cast. As I watched the fly float along, our guide said, "Missed another one." A few moments later he added, "Just missed another." I couldn't believe it! Because no matter how hard I tried, I couldn't spot one fish hitting that fly!

Frustrated, I handed my pole to our guide and suggested that he show me what he meant. Then I stepped back and smiled with quiet assurance. His cast was in the exact same spot mine had been. Instantly, a big trout hit the fly! My son doubled over in laughter as the guide handed me back the pole and reminded me there were many fish out there waiting for a chance at a fly. I stepped forward, sensing it was my turn to catch the next one. My cast fell in the exact same spot, and I leaned into the wind, taut with anticipation. Although I'm not a fishing pro, I have caught many fish in my lifetime, and this was getting a little embarrassing.

About thirty seconds later I heard him say those impossible words again: "You missed another one." I couldn't believe it! I hadn't felt the slightest vibration in my pole. I thrust the pole toward the guide, and another trout made a fool out of me with his very next cast. I couldn't stand it any longer, and I asked him to let me in on his secret.

For the first time, he smiled. "The fish here are real smart. Because they live in a catch-and-release section of the river, they've been caught scores, maybe *hundreds* of times. They watch that fly go by, touch it to the front part of their lips, and spit it out immediately if there's anything hard. It only takes a split second. The reason you haven't caught one yet isn't because they haven't taken the fly, but because you haven't developed the touch to set the hook in that split second before they 'quick spit' it back into the water!"

Like those trout, we need to develop an incredible sense of awareness. Temptation may be seeking to hook us, so we need to learn to spit it out so quickly it never gets "set" in our lives. Those trout were like the people mentioned in the book of Hebrews: "Because of practice [they] have their senses trained to discern good and evil" (Hebrews 5:14, NASB).

May you and I become so practiced in the ways of holiness that we can discern immediately when the desires of our heart are going after that which will cause us to sin. How can you defeat temptation? Practice your "quick spit"!

The secret to stage four: *Decide ahead of time not to sin and never permit yourself to think of one good reason to commit the sin, and you'll never make the choice to sin.*

STAGE FIVE: THE BIRTH

In most cases, after a person has conceived sin by deciding to do it, the sin is quickly committed, or "birthed." In other cases, a period of "incubation time" exists between the conception and the birth of the sin, during which the believer has one last opportunity to change his mind and forgo the sin. During this window of opportunity, the Holy Spirit frequently works powerfully, pleading with the believer to stop the sin. Conviction floods the heart, and the Lord once more extends mercy by offering the believer one last opportunity for deliverance.

The secret to stage five: *If you're about to commit the sin, force yourself to submit to the conviction of the Holy Spirit and abort the sin before it's too late.*

STAGE SIX: THE GROWTH OF SIN

Sin grows. If you've given in to anger, eventually anger grows into rage. If you've given in to lust, lust grows. If you've given in to the love of money, the love of money grows. Sin is never satisfied with only one occurrence.

Sin is not only addictive, it's like a living organism that grows from conception to birth to full maturity. Between birth and maturity are all the intermediate stages of any other organism, as sin grows and develops. One sin grows and expands into the next sin and then the next. Sin is never satisfied to remain static but quickly degenerates into deeper, sustained sin. Sin seeks to rule in the life of every man and woman.

The secret to stage six: *Every sin you commit digs your grave deeper. Therefore, never believe the lie that says "Just let me sin this one more time and then I'll give it up." Every sin strengthens itself against you for the next time.*

STAGE SEVEN: THE DEATH

The power and presence of sin grow steadily as the believer repeatedly chooses to sin. Over time and through repeated defeat, the believer experiences a most destructive trend. In the earlier stages of practicing this sin, he could simply choose to stop it; but in the later stages he can barely resist it, even when he summons all his determination and prays sincerely.

Although some teach that a true believer cannot fall prey to the power of sin, the Bible teaches that you can. And everyone's experience validates that it happens. A whole book could be written on this subject, but here are a few passages from Romans to stimulate your own study:

Therefore do not let sin reign in your mortal body, that you should obey it in its lusts. (Romans 6:12)

For sin shall not have dominion over you. (Romans 6:14)

Do you not know that to whom you present yourselves slaves to obey, you are that one's slaves whom you obey, whether of sin leading to death, or of obedience leading to righteousness? (Romans 6:16)

For just as you presented your members as slaves of uncleanness, and of lawlessness leading to more lawlessness, so now present your members as slaves of righteousness for holiness. (Romans 6:19)

Paul makes it clear that sin can certainly reign in the believer's life. That's why he commands us to not allow it. Sin can have dominion for an extended period of time over any believer who continually succumbs to its temptations. Note the phrase "sin leading to death," which pictures sin as spreading like cancer in the life of the believer who lives under its dominion.

What does this "death" look like? It's a slow darkness that creeps like the morning fog over the landscape of a person's life. Joy, peace, and assurance slowly depart—to be replaced by depression, anxiety, and doubt. I have found that believers who experience an extended period of dominion under the harsh taskmaster of sin eventually begin to doubt everything, until they doubt even their own salvation.

As the believer continues to sin again and again, his eyes slowly become clouded. He cannot see that which he used to see quite easily. A believer who is blinded, or hardened, to the truth is often in terrible bondage. And sin keeps pushing until the believer loses all self-control in that area of his life:

And a servant of the Lord must not quarrel but be gentle to all, able to teach, patient, in humility correcting those who are in opposition, *if God perhaps will grant them repentance, so that they may know the truth, and that they may come to their senses and escape the snare of the devil, having been taken captive by him to do his will.* (2 Timothy 2:24–26)

Although some may teach that this passage doesn't apply to believers, the context proves that it does. Can a believer actually be taken captive by Satan to do his will in an area of his life? Absolutely. Many times I have worked with believers around our world who have come to me in desperation, seeking freedom from terrible bondage to sin. Their eternal salvation isn't the problem; rather, they have lost their way and fallen into the snare of the enemy.

People don't lose their salvation because of their sin—they only need to be freed from it and they will once again walk in holiness. That's why Paul tells the Romans who are under the dominion of sin to present themselves to the Lord and get under the dominion of righteousness. He doesn't tell them to get saved or to get saved again. Instead he tells Timothy to, in humility, correct them so they may come to their senses, know the truth, and break free from their terrible captivity.

The secret to stage seven: *Regardless of the degree of bondage you are under, the work of Christ is sufficient to set you free completely.*

You Can Defeat Temptation

I can think of few things more wonderful than watching this miracle of freedom from the dominion of sin take place in the life of a believer. I recently dealt with two men on this very issue. The first took four and a half hours before we knelt on the floor and wept as he finally came to his senses and the Lord broke the enemy's bond. The second one took less than an hour. You should have seen him and his wife the next morning. They were absolutely transformed!

Were these men true believers? Absolutely. Were they in bondage to the enemy in at least one particular area of their lives? Yes, and they were quick to admit that to me. Were their minds blinded? Certainly. Were they walking in darkness in this area of their lives? Without question. Were they captive to the enemy's will in this area? Both men described themselves using the words *helpless* and *bondage*.

The first was a pastor of fifteen years. Surprising? The second was a pastor of *forty-five* years. Don't ever believe that it can't happen to you, friend. The result of a choice to willfully sin has terrible and destructive consequences, which can destroy your life and the lives of the people around you.

No sin, no bondage can ever hope to overpower our mighty Deliverer.

But the good news, the phenomenal news, is that the precious blood of Jesus has set us free. First John 3:8 says this powerfully: "For this purpose the Son of God was manifested, that He might destroy the works of the devil." Freedom from all bondage to sin is provided by

the death and resurrection of Jesus and is the full right and privilege of every believer.

Friend, if you are in bondage to sin in your life right now, I want to encourage you. It is never too late to turn around, repent, come to your senses, and be released from the clutches of your enemy.

Your life can be fully cleansed. Your conscience can be clean. No sin, no bondage, and no devil can ever hope to overpower our mighty Deliverer, the Lord Jesus! Go back to chapter five and carefully work your way through the ten steps of deep cleansing. If you continue to struggle, go see your pastor or another godly person. Reveal your sin and ask for their help.

The Lord always gives grace to those who humble themselves and seek His cleansing.

Chapter 8

The World's Toughest Temptation

We are half-hearted creatures, fooling around with
drink and sex and ambition, when infinite joy is offered us.
Like an ignorant child who wants to go on making mud
pies in a slum because he cannot imagine what is meant
by the offer of a holiday at the sea, we are far too easily pleased.

C. S. LEWIS

In a recent meeting with a group of forty men, I asked what they felt were the three biggest temptations men face today. A man in the first row called out, "Number one, sex; number two, sex; number three, sex!" The room exploded with laughter. They laughed because it's true. In a recent survey, Christian men were asked to list the sins they struggled with most. Sexual immorality of one kind or another was far and away the sin that appeared most on their lists.

Lest you think this is a men-only problem, evidence increasingly shows that women are as tempted as men to sin sexually—from fantasizing sexual encounters to engaging in physical immorality. When I discussed this problem with a businessman recently, he laughed and pointed out, "For every sexual affair in my office or one-night fling on a business trip, I've noticed there's always a woman just as involved as the man!"

Sexual immorality is clearly the most widespread and destructive of all sins in our culture, yet it is rarely preached about or openly discussed in Christian circles. Left unchallenged, it eventually rules and ruins the lives of those under its dominion. Soon these men and women lose all hope of ever being free and clean again, and they slide into a dark, solitary prison of defeat and despair.

DOES GOD UNDERSTAND YOUR SEX DRIVE?

Let me ask you a strategic question: Do you think the Lord really understands your sex drive? Or do you believe He created everything about you, including your sex drive, but something went wrong in the process? Or perhaps you think the Lord created man and woman with strong sex drives but just enjoys watching them squirm.

All but the first of these couldn't be further from the truth. The Lord indeed created sex and our sex drive as a wonderful gift for many good reasons. But this is a delicate subject, so we need to keep three things in mind as we explore the topic.

First, we need to remain biblical. The Bible doesn't leave us in the dark. Instead it reveals the very heart and mind of God on the subject of sexuality and sexual immorality. A New Testament passage on sexual immorality will be unashamedly presented here as God's answer to the problem. I will not add current psychological or sociological comment to the Word of God.

Second, we need to be straightforward. Of all the chapters in this book, this was the most difficult to write and may be the most difficult to read. Sexuality is a very private matter. In struggling with how to deal with this sensitive issue, the Lord reminded me that what He said and how He said it in Scripture reveal exactly what He wants us to know—nothing more and nothing less. Therefore, we are going to deal with one primary passage written under the inspiration of God through Paul to a local church. When this letter was received, it was read out loud to the whole congregation. Paul wrote these words to a mixed audience, and the audience heard them in a public setting. Therefore, I will be as straightforward as the Bible.

Third, we need to stay focused. This chapter is about dealing with sexual temptation and is not designed as a systematic attack on the ills of our culture. If you feel that I am glossing over any social issues, remember our focus: What does the Bible teach about sexual immorality?

Also, space does not permit a broad and complete presentation of love in marriage, so this chapter is narrowly focused on what one primary New Testament passage teaches on God's solution to the problem of sexual immorality.

TEACHING GOD'S STANDARD FOR SEXUAL CONDUCT

Many Christians are unclear in their minds about what is and isn't holy behavior when it comes to their sexuality. Years ago, when I was speaking at a Bible teaching conference in a hotel, I experienced in a most amazing way the deep confusion regarding God's standards of sexuality.

On the second afternoon, many of the attendees were scattered around the hotel swimming pool, talking and discussing what they were learning. I engaged several of them in conversation, asking each of them to share their names, where they were from, and what brought them to the conference. One young woman announced she had flown in from another state with her boyfriend. She added that her boyfriend couldn't be with us, as he was in their room watching the baseball game. I smiled and asked her if he was attending the course as well, but she said, "No, he's not a Christian yet, but he wanted to come with me."

At that point, no one around that previously animated group seemed to be breathing any longer. I asked the young woman if she and her boyfriend had spent the night together, and she unashamedly said they had and had been living together for almost two years.

"Are you a Christian yet, or still on the way to Christ?" I asked.

"Oh, I've been a Christian for almost five years and really growing." She mentioned her home church and enthusiastically said she really enjoyed her Sunday school class.

I shot up a quick prayer for grace and asked, "How do you think God feels about the two of you living together?"

"It's fine!" she answered with a bright smile. "I think he's going to become a Christian. And when he does, then we'll be married."

"If God were to say you shouldn't have sex or live together before you are married," I continued, "what do you think you would do?"

By her body language it was clear that the very notion had never occurred to her. "Well, I would have to ask my boyfriend to leave. It would be hard, but I love God and would do what He asked. Why?"

I looked around our little group, but as you might expect, a

Bible had not been among anyone's swimming paraphernalia that hot afternoon. I said to her, "How about going up to your room and bringing back the Gideon Bible? I'll show you something very important about the will of God for you and your boyfriend. I think you'll be very interested."

Off she went. No one around our pool circle seemed to have anything to say. Some were praying, as this was apparently an unexpected divine appointment. When the young woman returned with the Bible, I showed her some key passages and asked her to read them aloud for everyone else. In short order she saw what the will of God was with her own eyes.

We have neglected to teach the clear commands of God out of fear of rejection or ridicule.

Then, for the first time, she became uncomfortable—not because of the people gathered around but because of the convicting work of the Holy Spirit. She said, "Then what I'm doing is 'fornication'—and a big sin in God's eyes, right?"

I nodded and waited for the Holy Spirit to lead her. "Well," she said as her eyes flooded with tears, "then my boyfriend has to leave. We can't live together until we are married. Right?" I nodded in gentle affirmation. How kind the Lord was to lead her so gently to His will.

I will never forget what she said next: "I grew up in a totally non-Christian home. I didn't know anyone who was a Christian. All my friends slept together, so I never thought much about it. But I've been a Christian for *five years,* going to church almost every week. How come no one ever told me that sleeping together before you were married was a sin?"

At that moment, everyone around our group looked up. No one spoke as the conviction of the Lord moved from the sin of this young lady to the sin of believers everywhere who have neglected to teach the clear commands of God out of fear of rejection or ridicule. Something deep inside me broke when she asked that probing and painful question. Since then, I have not taken anything for granted in my teaching. May the Lord grant this same conviction to all who know His Word.

DEFINING SEXUAL IMMORALITY

What specifically is sexual sin? Listed below are the Bible's five major categories of sexual sin.

Sex Before Marriage

Generally, sex between unmarried people is called the sin of fornication. And sex before marriage with the person you marry later on is just as much fornication as sex with a person you don't intend to marry. Engaged couples are not married until they are legally wedded by a civil or religious authority, and until they consummate their marriage following the wedding service. Engaged couples who say "secret vows" to each other in order to engage in sexual relations before they are formally married are not married in the Lord's eyes and are still committing fornication.

Sexual Intercourse with Anyone but Your Spouse

After marriage, a sexual relationship with any person except the person you are married to is always sexual immorality.

Any Sexual Activity with Anyone but Your Spouse

Sexual immorality includes anything one person does with a person who is not his or her spouse for the purpose of sexual pleasure or satisfaction. This includes sexual activities undertaken with a consenting adult, with a child, with a family member, or with a hired sexual partner. All are immoral in the Lord's sight.

Anything Done by Yourself for the Purpose of Sexual Arousal

This general principle is of great assistance in helping a believer define whether he or she is moving into sexual immorality. The Bible directs the fulfillment of sexual desires toward the marriage partner. Purposely seeking sexual arousal or satisfaction with anyone or anything except a spouse is not within the will of God. This would include viewing pornography, calling "900" sex lines, visiting pornographic Internet sites, and attending massage parlors for the purpose of sexual arousal. Close and intimate relationships after marriage with a person of the opposite sex can also lead to emotional and sexual infidelity and should be avoided.

Lustful Thoughts

Jesus clearly defines lustful thoughts as sexual immorality in Matthew 5:28: "But I say to you that whoever looks at a woman to lust for her has already committed adultery with her in his heart."

Randy Alcorn says, "A relationship can be sexual long before it becomes erotic. Just because I'm not touching a woman, or just because I'm not envisioning specific erotic encounters, does not mean I'm not becoming sexually involved with her. The erotic is usually not the beginning but the culmination of sexual attraction."

Lustful thoughts are often spurred by lewd magazines, racy novels, movies and videos depicting nudity or sexual activity, and talk shows that glorify sexual immorality. These should be avoided.

Now that you know more about the Lord's standards for sexual conduct, how would you evaluate your related behavior in the sight of the Lord during the past few months? Have you been sexually pure? Have you pursued sexual arousal or pleasure with anyone or anything except your marriage partner? If you are not married, are you practicing celibacy both mentally and physically?

You may be feeling more than challenged in light of the Lord's standards for your behavior. At this point, you may be asking:

- What is God's answer to my sex drive?
- How do I handle my struggles with self-control?
- When sexual temptations arise, how can I defeat them?

You are about to read for yourself the remarkable—and perhaps shocking—revelation of the Bible's powerful answer to all three of these crucial questions.

THE LORD'S PROVISION FOR SEXUAL TEMPTATIONS

First Corinthians 7:2–5 gives us the Lord's answer to sexual temptation:

> But because of immoralities, each man is to have his own wife, and each woman is to have her own husband. The husband must fulfill his duty to his wife, and likewise also the wife to her husband. The wife does not have authority

over her own body, but the husband does; and likewise also the husband does not have authority over his own body, but the wife does. Stop depriving one another, except by agreement for a time, so that you may devote yourselves to prayer, and come together again so that Satan will not tempt you because of your lack of self-control. (NASB)

Read through this passage again slowly before we explore God's seven principles for defeating sexual immorality.

1. Each Person Should Marry

The Lord's provision for sexual immorality is to get married! This passage is the most direct revelation regarding God's plan to provide for our sex drives in a way that pleases Him. Therefore, marriage is to be considered holy and set apart unto Him.

But marriage couldn't really be the answer to all kinds of sexual immoralities, could it? What about pornography? How can marriage solve the temptations on the Internet? What about the temptations you face in the marketplace and while traveling away from home?

Marriage is the answer to immorality of all kinds. The words "each man is to have his own wife, and each woman is to have her own husband" are imperatives—positive commands which are to be obeyed unless God uniquely circumvents that norm with the rare gift of singleness. Why? Because marriage is meant to satisfy the sex drive.

At the time of the New Testament writing (and for hundreds of years afterward) marriages occurred closer to the age of puberty. Marriage permitted the blossoming sex drive to be fulfilled and not frustrated. Today, however, marriage is usually postponed until later in life due to modern educational, vocational, and financial pressures. The longer a human being postpones marriage past puberty, the more sexual temptations he or she will naturally have to face.

As a result, many individuals give in to their sexual temptations and choose to engage in sexual immorality of some form. By finding sexual release outside the marriage union, millions of singles are circumventing the God-given pressure for a mate, bypassing the normal marriage timetable. I have spoken at many singles conferences in my lifetime, and sadly, I can tell you that the majority of Christian singles are sexually active and therefore sexually immoral. Because they have found release for their God-given drives in a God-condemned manner, their personal marital clock has been radically affected.

Marriage is the answer to immorality of all kinds.

I'll never forget a conversation I had at a Bible conference in Phoenix. A morning session on sexual immorality had surfaced some intense emotion and discussion, and on my way back to my room a long-time friend fell into step beside me. "Bruce," he said, "I just don't know what to tell these younger guys anymore."

"What do you mean?" I asked, surprised because he had been discipling men for almost half a century.

"Well," he continued, looking kind of sheepish, "some of these guys have real sexual problems—with temptations and immoral things—and I can't identify with all that. My wife has always met all my sexual needs, and well, I just don't have any frustrations in that area."

I can still remember the impact of his honest and vulnerable words. I stopped right in the middle of that hallway and looked him directly in the eyes. "You have nailed the Bible's answer! You are *not* sexually immoral, not only because of your commitment to Christ, but because you have practiced God's perfect plan against temptations to sexual immorality—sex in marriage!"

Then I turned to this very verse in my Bible and said, "Show it to them; teach it to them. Don't mince any words, and don't back down one inch. But make sure you share how it's worked so wonderfully in your fifty-year marriage!"

2. Married Partners Are to Fulfill Their Sexual Duties

Paul writes, "The husband must fulfill his duty to his wife, and likewise also the wife to her husband" (1 Corinthians 7:3, NASB). The Lord anticipated this particular problem. Because although marriage is the only God-approved release for one's sex drive, it doesn't provide that release for many men and women. You see, *marriage* isn't the answer; *sex* within marriage *is!*

The Bible teaches that marriage is a delight as well as a duty. A duty is a moral or legal responsibility or obligation that arises from one's position. It is the duty of each married person to meet the sexual needs of his or her partner.

Paul makes it clear that the husband has a duty to his wife, just as the wife has a duty to her husband. It isn't the husband's duty to have sex with his wife if *he* wants it; but it *is* his duty to respond to his wife if *she* wants to have sex—and vice versa. The duty does not belong to the person who *initiates* the sex, but to the person who *responds*. For instance, let's say the husband makes sexual overtures to his wife. The Bible teaches that it is her responsibility as his wife to have sex. Why? Because in this case, the husband has a sexual drive seeking fulfillment, and it's her duty to make sure his needs are met. Therefore, whenever your spouse initiates sex in your direction, make sure you keep in mind that you are under God-given direction to meet your spouse's sexual needs.

Paul also makes a point here of using the word *fulfill,* meaning to make full, to bring to completion, to develop the full potential. Since our duty in this area is related to our spouse's parallel obligation not to commit sexual immorality, the actions of both partners should satisfy the sexual needs in such a way that each partner would say they are fully satisfied.

Which of the two marital partners must be the one to decide if the sexual drives or desires are completely satisfied? The one initiating sex. In other words, the only way a husband can know if he has "fulfilled his duty" as a husband is to ask his wife, "Are your sexual needs fully satisfied? Do you feel loved?"

After counseling hundreds of couples over the past thirty years, I can promise you that it is the rare married couple who understands and practices this biblical principle. Remember, the sense of duty being fulfilled is in reference to your partner's needs, not yours. The Bible conclusively puts the responsibility to satisfy sexual needs under the obligation of the marriage partner. Therefore, in general terms, the married partner should view his or her duty as being whatever it takes (but is not illegal or immoral) to satisfy the sexual needs of his or her partner.

I'll never forget talking to a man in a parking lot after a holiness conference. His marriage had ended in divorce after he committed adultery numerous times. He was a broken man, and his eyes filled with tears as he said, "If only my wife had believed what the Bible teaches about sex in marriage, my life might not be the total wreck it is today. She protected and ruled her body, using it as a carrot or a stick in my life. Oh, I know committing adultery isn't my wife's fault; it's mine. But if she would have had sex with me more than once a month, this might never have happened. She turned me away hundreds of times in our marriage, until I didn't even bother to risk the pain of rejection again. I looked elsewhere. The amazing thing is, I didn't *want* to go anywhere else. I loved my wife—but she decided if I had sex with another woman, it proved I didn't love her. So she divorced me. I think how life could have been so very different if she had known and believed Scripture."

There are always two sides to every story, but I wonder if that wife knows the part she played in her husband's immorality. She directly withheld from her husband the only acceptable fulfillment of his sexual needs. That's the point of this passage—because of sexual immorality, she was to fulfill her duty. They both sinned gravely by disobeying the Lord's clear command.

3. *The Lord Gave Authority Over Your Body to Your Spouse*

Paul writes, "The wife *does not have authority over her own body*, but the husband does. And likewise the husband does not have authority over his own body, but the wife does" (1 Corinthians 7:4). When I fully came to grips with what is said in this verse, I began to understand the Lord's extensive provision He made for our sexual purity. This verse reveals the remarkable extent to which a husband and wife are to fulfill their duty regarding the sexual needs and desires of their partner.

God sovereignly takes something away at the point of marriage and gives it as a heavenly wedding present to your spouse. The Lord doesn't ask you if He can take it, and the Lord doesn't ask you if you want it. Sovereignly, the Lord takes the authority you have had over your own body as a single individual and removes it from you for as long as you live. The term *authority* in this passage literally means to have rights over or exclusive claim to. In uncomplicated terms, God gave my body to my wife and I have nothing to say about it.

Of course, discussion on this point raises several questions which must be carefully thought through in the life of each couple. In my discussions on this topic with many couples, three misconceptions seem to inevitably surface.

First, some people believe that sex is inherently dirty or sinful or given solely for the purpose of conceiving children. The Bible consistently teaches that sex is a gift from God, that you are to relish your sexual life as a couple—independent of having children—and that to be naked before your spouse is nothing to be ashamed about. The Lord wouldn't exhort you to "fulfill your sexual duty" and give your body to your spouse if sex within marriage were less than holy in any way. Marriage is holy because the Lord said it is; He set that relationship aside from every other relationship in the world.

A second misconception is that sex is either a reward or punishment. The Lord already gave authority over your body to your spouse, so sex is not to be withheld as a punishment or bestowed as a reward. Sex is not to be offered solely because your spouse has been kind, given you a nice gift, come home on time, cleaned the house, not overspent the charge card, or in some other way "deserves" sex. Neither can sex be withheld because a spouse has been unkind, harsh, forgetful, late, messy, or a spendthrift. God takes sex out of the "reward and punishment" arena and places it within your spouse's authority to enjoy or not enjoy.

A third misconception about sex is that it is an optional part of marriage depending upon one's moods or preferences. Most married people tend to consider sexual intimacy within their authority rather than within their spouse's. Many don't initiate sexual intimacy due to a fear of rejection—yet the Bible bluntly takes the option of rejection away. The proverbial excuses about headaches or fatigue or "Come on, we had sex last night!" fall under the false mindset that my body is mine alone and I can do with it as I please. When the Christian married couple fully embraces God's delegation of authority, their marriage undergoes an amazing and wonderful transformation.

This clear teaching from the Bible goes directly against the independent self-orientation of our modern culture. Christian marriages are to be characterized by selfless love. No wonder the Lord's primary solution for sexual immorality is so widely abandoned! Yet it is the will of God that married men and women should experience satisfaction and fulfillment—*not* frustration and disappointment—in their sexual lives.

4. Do Not Deprive One Another of Sex

Paul writes, "*Stop depriving one another,* except by agreement for a time, so that you may devote yourselves to prayer, and come together again so that Satan will not tempt you because of your lack of self-control" (1 Corinthians 7:5, NASB).

Just imagine this happening at 6:00 P.M. as you arrive home from work. You walk in the back door and announce, "Wow, am I hungry! I can't wait until dinner." Your spouse looks up and says, "What are you talking about? I made you breakfast and you ate it. Then you went out for lunch, and you ate again. Now you want me to make dinner for you? What are you, some kind of glutton?"

How would you feel at that moment? And your spouse continues, "You're always thinking of yourself. *Your* hunger. *Your* timetable. You are so selfish!"

Now this will probably never happen to you. Why? Because everyone knows that breakfast and lunch do not even begin to fill your need for food at supper time. No one would call you selfish because of your God-given desire for food at mealtimes, would they? So if a man had sex the night before, why does he somehow feel selfish for desiring it two nights in a row? Or why should we look down upon a woman who desires sex more than her husband does?

Is the need for food God-given and therefore good? Is the need for sex God-given and therefore good? The answer must be an equally strong yes to both questions.

The will of God is that married men and women should experience fulfillment in their sexual lives.

Why then is there so much confusion and emotional frustration surrounding the sex drive and very little surrounding our need for food?

First of all, the food drive can be fulfilled without anyone else's participation. Only minutes ago, I went upstairs and made myself a cup of coffee and a piece of toast. I didn't require the help of my wife or anyone else. The sex drive, on the other hand, requires the active participation of another person (the spouse) every single time if it is to be fulfilled according to God's Word.

Another reason is that just about everyone gets hungry at least three times a day. In most cultures, everyone expects to eat a breakfast, lunch, and dinner. And most people get hungry at about the same time. The sex drive, on the other hand, varies wildly among men and women and even changes over time. This represents a sovereign choice by our Creator God, that all marriages will experience a certain disequilibrium regarding our built-in sexual clocks.

I can't tell you the number of men who feel "selfish" because of their God-given sex drives. But the need for sex in varying frequencies has nothing to do with men or women but everything to do with God. Men are no more "selfish" because they require sex more frequently than women are "selfless" because they need sex less frequently.

However, whenever I teach this truth, a few of the women in the audience become defensive. "If I let my husband have sex as often as he wanted," they protest, "we'd have sex every single night!"

Just read that sentence once more, but this time from the Lord's perspective.

Now return with me for a moment to the illustration of our desire for food. Let's say that when the wife came home from the office for dinner, even though it was her husband's turn to cook, he not only hadn't prepared anything but had locked up all the food in the house. What would she be tempted to do? Right. Go *out* to eat. If this happened again, she may start looking for food in someone else's kitchen. Or she might begin stashing food beneath her bed or in the back of her dresser drawers.

I realize the difficulty for many presented with this biblical passage. For those who have denied their spouse's sexual advances and held back their bodies over and over again, this verse has drastic implications: "Stop depriving one another...so that Satan will not tempt you because of your lack of self-control."

The word translated "deprive" literally means "do not rob one another," or "do not defraud one another." Defrauding occurs in a marriage when one partner cheats his spouse of what is properly hers. If you withhold your body when your partner seeks sex, it is biblical fraud.

I'll never forget what happened after I taught this to about five hundred Christian leaders. Many were weeping tears of repentance. One dignified woman came to me after everyone had left. Her eyes were bloodshot and her pain no longer hidden. She said, "I had no idea how I have been defrauding my husband all of our married life. I told him no for every reason under the sun just to avoid having sex. Finally, he stopped asking, and I fear he's gone elsewhere. I have sinned greatly against God and against my husband. Is it too late?"

Oh, what a precious time we had together that evening as the rain poured outside and the cleansing waters of God's Word washed over her life. When she turned to leave, she was a different woman. As she left she said, "My husband may have a heart attack, but starting tonight, I'm going to more than fulfill my duty to meet his sexual needs!"

5. You May Deprive Each Other of Sex Under Only Four Conditions

What are the exceptions? Does Scripture tell me I have to have sex *every* time my partner wants it?

> Stop depriving one another, *except by agreement for a time so that you may devote yourselves to prayer,* and come together again so that Satan will not tempt you because of your lack of self-control. (1 Corinthians 7:5, NASB)

Fortunately, the Bible doesn't leave us in the dark about this most important issue and outlines four conditions whereby one marriage partner can deny the other's request to have sex.

Sex Can Be Withheld When You Both Agree

You can't decide by yourself to deprive your spouse of sex. Both of you must agree not to have sex in order to fit into this exception.

Here's how this may work in real life. Let's say that last night your spouse rolled over in bed and made sexual advances. Because you had a long and exhausting day, you said, "I'm really tired tonight. Would it be all right with you if we waited until tomorrow night? If not, sweetheart, you know that tonight is okay, too. What would you like?"

Biblically speaking, who has the final say in this decision? The initiating partner always has the final say. If your spouse wants sex even after hearing your request, he or she still has authority over your body. However, just because your body belongs to your spouse doesn't mean you don't have the freedom to negotiate! When the initiating partner hears a willing but tired attitude of acceptance rather than rejection, understanding should be forthcoming.

Sex Can Be "Deprived" When You Both Agree to Delay It for a Time

Whenever a couple mutually agrees to deprive one another of sexual intimacy, the two must agree when they *will* have sex. To agree only to "not tonight" would not be following the biblical pattern. Scripture uses a very specific Greek word for time here which means a *specific period* of time.

Sex Can Be Set Aside to Devote Yourselves to Prayer

This certainly presents a clear and rather unusual reason for depriving yourself of sexual relations in modern society. The only biblical purpose for depriving yourselves of sex is to devote yourselves to sharing a spiritual focus in your marriage.

Sex Can Be Deprived Until the Two of You Agree to Come Together Again

The Bible quickly brings us back to the reality that sexual intimacy is to be the norm and never the exception.

6. If You Deprive Each Other, You Open Yourself to Attack

First Corinthians 7:5 blatantly states that in sexual matters you must come together after an agreed-upon time of sexual abstinence or you will open yourself up to satanic attack. After a period of time without sex, you are to come together again. If you don't, Satan will come against you with temptations to commit sexual immorality. The longer sex is postponed and the marital partners have not yet come together, the greater the risk of temptation.

7. You Lack Self-Control When You Deprive Each Other of Sex

What happens to married individuals when they don't have sex for a period of days? Satan tempts you, taking advantage of your lack of self-control. Depriving your spouse of sexual relations results in more than immediate, short-lived frustration. Continued postponement of sexual relations within a marriage places very real and unnecessary pressure on a spouse.

ENJOYING THE GIFT OF SEX

One of the realities of my ministry is travel away from home. I have now visited more than seventy nations, speaking through translators in more than fifty languages. I can't tell you the number of men who have come up to me after a presentation on this subject, expressing their great appreciation for my forthrightness, especially with their wives present. Sometimes even the most courageous among us find it difficult and rather uncomfortable to speak openly of these things.

My wife and I were in the hotel lobby during a weeklong training conference when a woman came up to us and asked if she could share something rather personal. She said how much she appreciated the "sex talk" and that even though she had been happily married to her husband (who was in full-time pastoral ministry) for more than twenty-five years, many of the concepts we shared about men's and women's sexual needs were new and even surprising to her.

That woman, who was nearly sixty years old, told us how disappointed she was that neither her mother nor any other older woman had ever communicated such a vital piece of information to her. She kind of smiled, broke eye contact with me, and said, "You know, Darlene, now that I know the truth, I will never let my husband out of the house before a trip away from home without the special gift that only I can give—even if he isn't in the mood! It's not just his present mood I'm concerned about; it's his mood tomorrow night when I won't be around that concerns me. I want to remain the only person he's tempted to seek that gift from!"

PART THREE

Habits of Holiness

Chapter 9

Pursuing Holiness

*We cannot say no to temptation without
saying yes to something far better.*

Erwin W. Lutzer

*E*very word in this book to this point has been written to prepare you for this chapter. By now, you understand that holiness means separation, that it must include separation from the secular and to the sacred, and that it must be defined by the standards of the Lord as given to us in His Word.

By now, you also understand that positional holiness means how the Lord views you the moment you accept His Son's sacrificial death for your sins; presentation holiness means that because of the compassions and mercies of the Lord, you have committed your whole life to Him and His service; and progressive holiness means that you constantly cleanse yourself from all that the Lord would consider to be unholy.

However, we've barely discussed what normally comes to mind when you think of holiness—Christlike conduct and character. In Ephesians 4:22–24, Paul ascribes a specific order to progressive holiness.

> That *you put off,* concerning your former conduct, the old man which grows corrupt according to the deceitful lusts, and be renewed in the spirit of your mind, and that *you put on* the new man which was created according to God, in true righteousness and holiness.

Unfortunately, many of us miss this biblical pattern and experience repeated defeat and even despair regarding our sincere attempts at personal holiness. The pattern to be followed is this: First, unholiness is to be cleansed; second, holiness is to be pursued. Although the Lord is pleased with all attempts at pursuing righteousness, the Bible alerts us to the fact that existing *unholiness* can prevent us from growing in holiness.

Pursue holiness by first cleansing all known unholiness.

In other words, you must tear out the dirty carpet before attempting to lay down the new carpet. "Put off" before you "put on." Depart from iniquity and then pursue righteousness. Does this mean we should never pursue the positive characteristics of righteousness first? No. But a truly biblical perspective would go something like this: Pursue holiness by first cleansing all known unholiness; when all known unholiness is washed away, then focus more directly on pursuing holiness.

When believers seek the positive attributes of holiness while permitting major areas of sin to remain, the Lord may regard even our positive acts as sinful. Why? Because we may be rationalizing our existing sin by thinking that our devotional life or positive acts of service may cause the Lord to "forget," or at least "wink at," our existing sins.

Again and again, the prophets declared the Lord's displeasure with the nation of Israel for their ritualistic attempts at obedience while daily practicing major sin. Their sin negated their obedience. Seeking the Lord in some areas while rebelling in others may defeat the whole process.

Christ was clear about which aspect of holiness should receive our attention first:

> "If you bring your gift to the altar, and there remember that your brother has something against you, leave your gift there before the altar, and go your way. *First* be reconciled to your brother, and *then* come and offer your gift." (Matthew 5:23–25)

Always seek to cleanse yourself from all unholiness as the first step in pursuing holiness. In other words, pursue holiness first by cleansing yourself of sin, and then pursue it further by adding habits of holiness. This is a central truth missing from the minds of many believers. Revival *begins* with repentance and cleansing and then *breaks forth* as we develop closer intimacy with Christ.

The Second Part of Progressive Holiness

The first half of progressive holiness focuses on helping you eliminate all the negatives from your life, whereas the second half focuses on helping you add all the positives. Both actions are *processes* rather than *events*, and both endure throughout your lifetime.

But don't fall prey to the idea that at no time can you be fully cleansed. The Bible commands us to work in that direction by departing from the ways of the world until the process is complete—at least for the time being. Although you've completed the process once, as long as you are in the world, you will later need to repeatedly work through the same process.

The fact is that the heart of man is deceitfully wicked. And despite the teachings of some, the Bible explicitly says that man is *not* basically good; instead, God's Word tells us that "the heart is deceitful above all things, and desperately wicked" (Jeremiah 17:9). When we obey the Lord and cleanse ourselves from all unrighteousness, we aren't immediately filled with all holiness; we are merely not unholy at that moment.

Remember, holiness is not simply an absence of unholiness. That's why the Bible exhorts us to deal with both sides of the holiness equation: Cleanse yourself and pursue righteousness. Put off the old man and put on the new man.

Conduct that is holy is characterized by the absence of sin and the presence of righteousness. The second half of progressive holiness is therefore the active and enduring pursuit of all that is Christlike.

THE DISTURBING TRUTH ABOUT HOLY HABITS IN THE CHURCH

I'll never forget the time I moved to a new city and visited a church that had been recommended to me. Four hundred adults attended service there each Sunday morning. On Wednesday night I visited the prayer meeting. The pastor was preaching in the main sanctuary, but the prayer meeting was nowhere in sight. In a small back-corner room I finally found the prayer meeting. Only four godly women about my mother's age met there weekly. Not coincidentally, there was very little interest in holiness among the congregation at large. Nor was there much life to be found there.

The next time you are together with someone who prays a lot, ask if he or she has experienced many seasons of personal cleansing. This person will probably just smile and nod. Here's some of what I've discovered in my own observations in thirty-plus years of ministry:

- Not counting prayers at meals or at church-related functions, the average born-again believer prays less than two minutes per day.
- When you don't count reading the Bible at a Christian function, the average born-again believer reads the Bible less than three minutes per day.
- The average born-again Christian donates less than 3 percent of his total gross income to Christian causes.

Do these statistics surprise or shock you? Probably not. And if you are uncomfortable with those statistics, do they describe your

Christian walk too closely? If so, this section of the book has been written for you.

Not only does the Lord desire you to break free from a shallow spiritual life, but in your heart, so do you!

By Their Fruits You Will Know Them

Not long ago I spent the afternoon with a senior student in one of our nation's most respected seminaries. I asked him how he had enjoyed his studies preparing for the ministry. He expressed appreciation for the many things he had learned there; but then he looked away and with a rather sad pensiveness spoke these words:

> I have one major disappointment: I never was taught and never learned how to walk with God. I learned theology, Bible, missions, Christian education, evangelism, apologetics, and other important things, and even had one semester on the spiritual life. But you know, I never really learned how to pray, never learned how to meet God, and never learned how to walk with God. And I fear that although I can "do ministry" better than when I entered three years ago, I really am not a more holy person than when I began. In fact, my heart is less tender and I pray less than when the whole thing started.
>
> Somehow, I was wrong. I thought seminary would teach me how to walk with God and lead me to become a man who was holy. It didn't. In fact, my teachers never seriously tried.
>
> I sat down a little while ago and just figured it out. Although I go to one of the nation's top three evangelical

seminaries—known for its emphasis on the spiritual life—
my entire seminary career of three intense years invested
less than 2 percent of that time on how to walk with God
and become a man of holiness.

Then he turned back to me and raised the questions I was afraid
he was going to ask. "Do you think, Dr. Wilkinson, my seminary
reflects the values of Jesus? Do you think my seminary models the
training that Jesus gave to His disciples? Do you think it's more
important to learn Greek and theology than how to walk with God,
how to pray, and how to be holy? Do you think that only 2 percent
of the New Testament epistles is about walking with God, walking
in the Spirit, praying, and living a life of holiness?"

What would you say to that young seminarian? As goes the
source, so goes the river. As go the seminaries and Bible colleges, so
go the pastors and missionaries. As go the pastors and missionaries,
so go our churches and Christian organizations. As go our churches
and Christian organizations, so go the believers.

Perhaps one last observation would be helpful. Let's say you
were new in town and wanted to find out about a church you were
interested in attending. But instead of asking the staff or members of
the church, you randomly knocked on eight doors all within walking distance of the church. What would the residents say when you
asked, "Could you please tell me about the church on the corner?"

I tried this one day. You should have heard the earful I received!
I heard about church splits, big arguments the whole town knew
about, the music director running away with the secretary, and the
pastor who kicked people out because it was "my way or the high-
way." As I slowly walked from the last front porch, the words of

Jesus came to mind: "Let your light so shine before men, that they may see your good works and glorify your Father in heaven" (Matthew 5:16).

You see, holiness makes its mark in the marketplace and town square—as does unholiness. Holiness spreads good works in every direction, influencing behavior and actions—as does unholiness. Jesus said:

> "Beware of false prophets, who come to you in sheep's clothing, but inwardly they are ravenous wolves. You will know them by their fruits.... A good tree cannot bear bad fruit, nor can a bad tree bear good fruit.... *Therefore, by their fruits you will know them.*" (Matthew 7:15–20)

Do you understand the Lord's logic? What is in a person—or a church—will come out. When a person is holy, he overflows with good works. When a church is holy, it overflows with good works, and everyone within driving distance knows about it.

The Fruits of the Church

Unfortunately, although there are notable exceptions, too many churches are known for the works of division, immorality, power-hungry leadership, and financial problems. When the community cannot name even one good work of the church in question, you can be sure the church is not committed to holiness.

Biblical holiness should overflow into the community in the form of good works. If the community knows nothing of a church's good works, then holiness is sorely lacking. Because as Jesus pointed out, fruit trees always bear fruit. Good trees bear good fruit, and evil trees bear evil fruit. If the community knows only of evil fruit, the church almost certainly cannot be holy in the Lord's eyes.

What then does a holy church really look like? Consider the life of a pastor who took over a fledgling church of two hundred when he was twenty. When he died at the age of fifty-eight, this same ministry had touched nearly the entire country. Let's look at some of the good fruit this one church bore in their community:

- Twenty-three mission stations actively ministering throughout the community
- Twenty-six branch Sunday schools throughout the community, including the poverty-stricken sections of downtown
- One thousand members working among the poor every Sunday evening
- Large and lasting revivals in the whole area
- Built a five thousand–seat church and fully paid for it
- Launched pastors college with more than a hundred pastors in training each year
- Held more than two hundred evening Bible classes each week in the area
- Launched and developed a large tract society
- Started an organization that distributed Christian books through house-to-house visits—in one year, more than nine hundred thousand homes were visited!
- Started more than two hundred new local churches throughout the area
- Constructed seventeen houses for widows and indigent women and donated all costs for the housing and food on an ongoing basis

- Launched and constructed an orphanage for four hundred children, supporting it entirely without government funding
- Donated tens of thousands of Christian books to missionaries and pastors all over the world
- Launched the Ladies' Benevolent Society and made clothes for the orphaned children of the city
- Baptized through its many ministries more than thirty-nine thousand new converts in just twelve years

Can you imagine what that community felt about the church and its humble servant, Charles H. Spurgeon? As the people of God there started *living* like the people of God, they bore good fruit via the *plan* of God.

Nearly every mark of visible holiness is missing in the vast majority of believers and churches these days. May we repent before the Lord, cleanse our hearts and actions, and pursue His holiness with all our hearts, souls, and might. When we do, not only will heaven shout in celebration, but so too will the ungodly living nearby glorify God, because they will see works worthy of their praise.

Friend, I urge you, as an alien and stranger in this world, to abstain from sinful desires that war against your soul. Live such a good life among those who do not yet know Christ that, though they accuse you of doing wrong, they may see your good deeds and glorify God on the day He visits us (see 1 Peter 2:11–12).

WHERE DO YOU STAND?

Examine yourself regularly to evaluate your progress toward holiness. As we have seen, this third stage of holiness is progressive, beginning at your spiritual birth and concluding at your physical death. Between these two points lie the only opportunities you have in all of eternity to grow in holiness.

Check your "holiness pulse rate" by reading through these seven overlapping seasons that reflect a growing spiritual maturity. Select the one that represents where you currently stand in the pursuit of personal holiness.

1. Repeatedly Fails in Attempts at Developing a Devotional Life

If you are experiencing considerable difficulty in establishing regular devotions, you are still at the starting line. The pull from existing sin in your life so weighs you down that you can only carry the load for a few days before giving up. Yet without regular time in the Word, you won't grow in holiness. Consider returning to chapter five and working through the painful but liberating ten-step cleansing.

2. Actively Serves the Lord in at Least One Regular Ministry

This second stage in the pursuit of holiness may in your case precede the previous stage, as it does for some Christians. The Lord always encourages His children to serve Him, and frequently this is an easier first step in moving toward Him. But if you are still merely attending church and remaining on the fringes, it's time to move closer to the center. Remember, the Lord saved you by His grace, but He saved you for His work: "For we are His workmanship, created in Christ Jesus for good works, which God prepared beforehand that we should walk in them" (Ephesians 2:10).

3. Aspires Deeply to Live a Much More Holy Life

Somewhere during his progressive movement toward holiness, the believer comes to a crossroads. In preparation, the Lord usually presents him with numerous small decisions that can move him either toward or away from holiness. If the believer continues to choose the pathway of obedience, eventually the Lord will bring him to the big decision of whether to knowingly and actively pursue holiness.

Think back for a moment to the introduction and the men who were asked to describe themselves with a few words—and consider whether *holiness* would be on their cards. Remember their aversion to the concept? Because holiness was not something they aspired to, they remained locked in the going-nowhere cul-de-sac of the spiritual life.

4. Abides with Christ Through Regular and Meaningful Devotions

By this time in the Christian's pilgrimage, his heart will have grown more fervent, and his hunger for the Lord will have grown considerably. Because of his desire for the Lord, he is willing to pay the required price of deep cleansings to experience more of the Lord. As a result of those cleansings, the Lord permits this believer to enjoy a more meaningful and satisfying relationship with Him.

At this point a major transition occurs: Devotions move out of the realm of *duty*, which requires considerable determination and discipline, and into the realm of *delight*, which means the payback far exceeds the effort. Devotions now become the high point of the believer's day.

5. Advances Faithfully in Obedience and Christlikeness

Once the Lord has fed His child through intimate devotions, He begins to call him more pointedly to deeper obedience. At this point, the believer desires more of the Lord so much that he is more than willing to do whatever the Lord requires. As his relationship with the Lord deepens, the believer becomes more attuned to His heart and walks more circumspectly, careful not to wound or quench the Holy Spirit.

Obedience for this individual is no longer a burden, undertaken only because the Bible tells him to do something. Rather, obedience becomes a joy because his closest friend and most compassionate Lord beckons him to be like Him. No longer does the believer rationalize whole areas of his life; indeed, he desires with deep determination to "put on" kindness, humility, meekness, longsuffering, and forgiveness (see Colossians 3:12–13).

6. Accelerates Investment of Time, Talent, and Treasure into the Lord's Work

By this time, so many threads of the believer's life have been woven together that he almost feels as if he is being carried along by the Lord—and he is! As the believer's heart is broken, cleansed, and redirected, he begins viewing life from heaven's perspective rather than earth's. What a dramatic difference this makes! Whole areas of his life that previously had been given high priority are now set aside because the believer recognizes their lack of eternal significance.

The Lord now invites the believer to enter deeper and deeper levels of holiness. During this season the believer realizes he is a steward of his life rather than the owner. As he submits to the Lord, he begins to redirect his time, talents, and treasure into the Lord's work. The believer's time becomes a precious commodity and he redeems the time as never before. The believer responsibly stewards his talents and money, seeking to multiply both for the Lord. He releases the Lord's money to Him—instead of using it for personal pleasure or hoarding it for fear of the future—and joyfully gives a growing percentage of his assets to the Lord and His service.

7. Abandons Everything to Know and Serve Christ

The "ultimate" state of holiness is complete conformity to the image of Jesus Christ in every area of life. In this final stage, all that the believer desires is to be one with Christ and to serve Him as Christ served His Father—completely, faithfully, and fervently. Paul recorded his seventh-stage attitude and actions in Philippians 3:8–14. Notice the depth of abandonment and intensity of intimacy and service:

> I also count all things loss for the excellence of the knowledge of Christ Jesus my Lord, for whom I have suffered the loss of all things, and count them as rubbish, that I may gain Christ...that I may know Him and the power of His resurrection.... I press on, that I may lay hold of that for which Christ Jesus has also laid hold of me...reaching forward to those things which are ahead, I press toward the goal for the prize of the upward call of God in Christ Jesus.

Reading this before, you may have wondered whether Paul's attitude is really realistic. Can we seek to follow in His footsteps and ultimately display the same attitudes, actions, and aspirations this side of heaven? The Bible answers this in the next few verses:

> Therefore let us, as many as are mature, have this mind; and if in anything you think otherwise, God will reveal even this to you. *Brethren, join in following my example,* and note those who so walk, as you have us for a pattern. For many walk, of whom I have told you often, and now tell you even weeping, that they...set their mind on earthly things. For our citizenship is in heaven, from which we also eagerly wait for the Savior, the Lord Jesus Christ. (Philippians 3:15, 17–20)

SOW HOLINESS NOW, REAP HOLINESS LATER

Holiness is not natural; it's supernatural. Holiness does not come as a result of one or two "crisis experiences"; it develops through years and years of godly living. The standards of holiness are clear and include "all your conduct" as Peter reminded us. Nestled deep within the words of Zacharias in Luke 1:74–75 is a remarkable prophecy regarding the work of Jesus for us:

> To grant us that we, being delivered from the hand of our enemies, might serve Him without fear, in holiness and righteousness before Him all the days of our life.

As you consider these verses, you'll see that they contain what may be the most succinct and remarkable summary in all the Bible of our life's goal concerning holiness: *to serve the Lord in holiness before Him all the days of our life!*

The longer I walk with the Lord, the more assured I am that one of the secrets of the spiritual life lies in the words "all the days of our life." Not "all the weeks of our life" or "all the months of our life" or "all the years of our life." Holiness grows most through daily life. Therefore, in this section the emphasis will be on specific daily practices that will generate guaranteed results in times of temptation.

Those words "guaranteed results" may sound a bit exaggerated, but they are as certain as the unchanging laws of sowing and reaping. What one sows, one will reap. Sow seeds in the holiness garden and you'll reap the fruit of holiness. Not some of the time, not most of the time, but *all* of the time. How encouraging!

Remember four main things as you begin this section:

1. The Time Between Sowing and Reaping Requires Patience

Patience isn't typically needed during the sowing or reaping, but in the time *between* the sowing and reaping. I remember planting my first vegetable seeds in our backyard as a child. I would race downstairs each morning, run out the back door, and head for the small, three-by-ten-foot garden, which seemed like a giant field to my young mind. I checked it each day just to see if my tomatoes, eggplants, and radishes had come up yet. After three days passed, I wanted to dig them up to make sure they were still there! Day after day nothing happened, and I became more and more discouraged. My wise father assured me that I must exercise patience, that they would come up when they were supposed to.

Paul knew all too well when he wrote Galatians 6:7, 9 the tendency among believers to grow impatient and lose faith:

> Do not be deceived, God is not mocked; for whatever a man sows, that he will also reap. And let us not grow weary while doing good [planting holiness seeds], *for in due season* [precisely on schedule] *we shall reap* [not *may* reap or *hope to* reap, but *shall* reap] *if we do not lose heart* [become discouraged because nothing has happened and stop sowing, watering, and weeding in the meantime].

Never doubt for a moment that if you continue in these holiness habits you will indeed enjoy a glorious and bountiful "harvest of holiness." The greater the harvest you desire, the more you must sow and continue to sow. God guarantees results in direct proportion to your sowing, but in a far greater amount. Do you know why? Because you always harvest many times more than you sow. Plant one tiny watermelon seed and plan to invite all your neighbors to help you enjoy the harvest.

2. The Reliability of Your Harvest Lies in the Quality of Your Seed

Plant tomato seeds and you will not grow cucumbers. If you seek holiness, then plant "holiness seeds." If you plant and water ineffective seeds, your payback will be discouraging and defeating. In my travels, I meet many disillusioned believers who, for one reason or another, have dropped out of the holiness pilgrimage. A large portion of them have trusted in "poor seed" to bear fruit in their lives.

Instead of seeking the good old standard packets of holiness seeds used by the church throughout the centuries, many believers seem drawn like moths to a flame to new methods for growing in holiness. John Bunyan's *The Heavenly Footman*, written in the mid-1600s, warns about this dangerous trend:

In the little time I have been a believer, I have observed that there is a great many running to and fro—some this way and some that way; yet it is to be feared that most of them are not on the right way. As a result, though they run as swift as the eagle can fly, they benefit nothing at all.

There is one who runs after quaking, another after ranting; still another runs after baptism, and another after independency…. Yet, it's possible that most all these…are running the wrong way.

Although there may be exceptions, the majority of believers who get sidetracked in their search for true holiness do so for one of three reasons.

First, many exhibit a propensity to seek a quick fix for an issue that does not respond to a quick fix. In other words, they are unwilling to practice the hard things of holiness, always seeking a simpler, easier, and quicker answer.

Second, some exhibit a weakness for making decisions on the basis of emotional experiences and "signs" that validate their unusual direction.

Third, others harbor a selfish ambition, driving them to find the deep things of God beyond their friends, family, and peers. Somewhere in this slide into delusion they believe they have uncovered a "lost truth" or previously unknown truth that God has entrusted only to them.

Friend, if this is you and you are still struggling to grow in holiness, adopt the tried-and-true habits outlined in the Word of God for the blessings of holiness.

3. Between Sowing and Reaping You Must Continue to Weed

In your pursuit of holiness, don't forget the inevitability of weeds! If you are new to the pursuit of holiness, expect many different kinds of weeds to surface. Why? Because up to now, your "field" was left open to the will of the land, and all kinds of thistles and weeds moved in.

During the first year of any garden, you must weed seemingly forever and sometimes with limited results. But the next year there will be fewer weeds and more fruit. The following year, even fewer weeds and greater quantities of fruit will appear. As that patch of ground is reclaimed by your attention and the weeds are ripped out, the ground slowly becomes totally devoted to your will and the seeds you plant. Instead of fighting to survive, your fledgling plants will experience nearly complete freedom to grow without distractions, diversions, or disasters.

4. Holiness Requires Sowing Multiple "Holiness Habits"

When our family first lived in the country, we planted only two things in our garden: watermelons and sweet potatoes. What a crop we had that year, and what a lesson we learned! Three weeks after the harvest of each of these crops, we all felt it would be fine if we *never* saw another sweet potato or watermelon. We gave bags of potatoes and melons to all of our friends and told each other that next year we'd be much wiser in what we planted. Sowing only one or two things leads to boredom.

There's often a real parallel in a sincere believer's search for holiness. By limiting himself to just one or two types of holiness practices, he literally brings boredom on himself. Instead, become a highly diversified holiness practitioner.

Recently, Darlene Marie and I talked about our various methods of holiness, both personally and as a couple. What a list we came up with as we outlined the various holiness tools that were meaningful in our lives!

Too often believers depend on only one or two methods to pursue holiness. May I encourage you to discover a few more and to rotate your crop? Give your "land" rest from one method and move on to another. Remember, holiness methods are merely tools. Whatever tools work for you are acceptable as long as they are either specifically biblical or widely practiced by godly men and women through the ages.

May not only your heart turn fully toward holiness, but may your *habits* begin to turn toward holiness as well! In the next chapter, join me in looking at the primary holiness habits you should master.

Chapter 10

Foundational Habits

*The serene, silent beauty of a holy life is the most powerful
influence in the world, next to the might of the Spirit of God.*

Blaise Pascal

ack at the turn of the century, Samuel Smiles expressed
the theme of this chapter: "Sow a thought, reap an act.
Sow an act, reap a habit. Sow a habit, reap a character.
Sow a character, reap a destiny."

In other words, character is the sum total of a person's habitual
traits and qualities. *Change your habits and in time you will change
your character. Therefore, to enjoy a life of holiness, change your habits
into habits of holiness.*

If you want to become a person whose character is holy, you
will have to identify and establish personal habits of holiness. The
more those habits are practiced, the more they will become part of
you, until they become the "whole" of you! Habits that become

involuntary are called "character qualities."

Moving toward holiness means changing negative habits of unholiness to positive habits of holiness. It also means that our understanding of becoming holy must move beyond generalities into specifics. Holiness isn't some vague, dreamlike existence. Holiness is specific and objective and is to be purposefully pursued by all who name the name of the Lord Jesus. He calls us to be holy in all our conduct (see 1 Peter 1:15), and He has provided everything we need for righteousness and godliness.

Because the Bible teaches that holiness is both a *position* as well as a *progression,* we must continue to think clearly about how holiness works. Holiness begins the moment we accept Jesus Christ as our personal Savior. At that time, the Lord separates us unto Himself as His children and members of His family. From that point forward, the Lord calls us to be transformed from glory to glory into the exact image of Jesus Christ. As time goes on, each of us should be exemplifying the traits of Christ's character—love, joy, peace, longsuffering, kindness, goodness, faithfulness, gentleness, and self-control.

Holiness is to be purposefully pursued by all who name the name of Jesus.

Most of our growth will be gradual and steady. Just as none of us can actually see the growth of a plant as it occurs, so is our growth in holiness small but significant. Leave time for its natural growth and one day you'll see a noticeable difference. In 2 Corinthians 7:1, Paul reminds us that we are to "cleanse ourselves from all filthiness...*perfecting holiness* in the fear of God." "Perfecting holiness" reflects the lifelong process of conforming ourselves to the image of Christ.

Remember, habits determine character, and character is not transformed unless habits of thought, belief, and behavior are changed. Just as you can't see a rose open its petals, so you may not actually "see" your character in Christ blossom. But look back on your life in a few months and you might not recognize yourself!

The Bible repeatedly exhorts us to practice these holiness habits, often with specific promises and benefits tied to them. And throughout the history of the church, Christians just like you and me have practiced these habits and have enjoyed the same beneficial results. You don't have to search for some magic words or secret initiation rite—these habits are obvious and within reach.

Try this experiment: Think of the most godly person you have ever met. Call him up and tell him you are in the middle of this book and that I encouraged you to call and ask one question: "What are the three biggest secrets to your walk with God?" More than likely, you'll find that they are basically the same spiritual disciplines that will be outlined in this chapter and the next.

ESTABLISH YOUR DEVOTIONAL HABIT

What is currently at the center of your life? Your work? Your marriage? Your family? Your church? Your leisure? Your money? Whatever it is, you must move it so that the Lord and your time with Him can become the central focus. The single most strategic change you can make is to put your daily "devotional habit" first on your priority list.

Half of the "devotional habit" is the word *devote*, which means "to set apart for a special and often higher end." The focus of daily devotions isn't the specific procedures you follow, but your relationship with the Lord. Because you are devoted to the Lord, you choose to dedicate priority time each day to Him and Him alone. And because He is the most important person in the world to you, you don't allow anyone or anything to take precedence. Here are a few tips for developing your devotional habit.

Select Your Devotional Habitat

The first key is to identify your favorite location in the house for your devotions. It should be quiet, comfortable, and as private as possible. In the Wilkinson home, "Darlene Marie's Place" is in the front room in her green rocker; "Jessica's Place" is in her bedroom; and "Bruce's Place" is in the basement, in the back corner.

In that corner sits my favorite blue chair, which a good friend from Colorado gave to me unexpectedly one afternoon. Just in front of it, along the wall, is a bookcase filled with my "spiritual life" books, journals, and my prayer journal. To the left is a lamp with a small table and at my right a large globe for praying for the world. For me, it's perfect.

As time passes, I have set apart this space to the Lord and dedicated it as the place where I rise to meet Him in the early morning. It has become filled with praise, worship, meditation, and intimate friendship.

Schedule a Normal Devotional Habit Time

I grew up as a staunch evening person. I was sure it made no difference to the Lord what time I decided to have my devotions, and I can remember defending my position rather vigorously in my early Bible college days. But one day, an older mentor and I were discussing this question and he asked me whether the spiritual giants of history had their primary devotions in the morning or evening. I had to admit that every one of them I was familiar with had them in the morning. But, I was quick to point out, that didn't prove anything!

When I said that, he folded his arms and smiled, not saying a word. Finally, when I had nothing else to say, he warmly but soberly said, "Bruce, until you stop defending your laziness and rise with the sun, you'll never meet Christ as you are seeking Him."

That friend proved absolutely correct. The early morning hours are the *holiness hours*. Over time, things changed and I have become a committed morning person. The Lord and I like to meet while the sun is yet rising.

This may mean you have to alter your routine, get to bed earlier, or at times live with less sleep. When priorities such as this change, a person's sleeping habit may suffer until he learns to discipline himself a bit more.

Whatever you eventually decide, *meet the Lord at the same time each day throughout the week.* As far as Saturday and Sunday are concerned, you might need to select different times. I don't get up early on Saturday, which usually means a more casual approach, and I wonder if perhaps the Lord enjoys this leisurely approach as well.

Remember not to fall prey to the temptation to become legalistic in your walk with the Lord. Your devotions should flex with the ebb and flow of your life to accommodate emergencies, exhaustion, and unexpected situations. Recently, while ministering at the Cove (Billy Graham's training center) in Asheville, North Carolina, I found myself counseling all day and very late into the evenings. On the last morning, I was so emotionally and physically exhausted that I rose early, pulled a large chair up to the fireplace, and enjoyed the presence of the Lord in quietness. I didn't follow my normal schedule, didn't pray through my prayer list, didn't write in my journal, and didn't even read my Bible. What did I do? I just sat in the presence of the Lord for an hour, worshiping and enjoying Him. Remember, devotions are for man, not man for devotions.

Structure Your Devotional Agenda for Each Day and Year

Nothing seems to ruin good intentions faster than not knowing what to do when you semistagger in the early morning hours to your "devotional place"—and then spend those precious moments in frustration trying to figure out what to do.

Take the complexity out of life! Develop a routine you follow each morning. I have discovered that the best way is to construct a new routine for each year based on what I discovered the previous year. Then, when I finally sit in my big blue chair with my orange juice and coffee, I don't waste a second. Unfortunately, it took me years to figure that out! I still remember the frustration of searching through the Bible trying to figure out what to read or what to pray. Now that never happens. It's wonderful!

What's the secret? Figure out what seems to work for you right now. Write it down on a sheet of paper, try it the next day, and revise it. It may take a couple of weeks to really zero in, but relax and don't try to figure it all out the first time. Get started, revise your list until you are comfortable, and then use it for the rest of the year. The point isn't how many things you do, but that whatever you do works for you.

TIPS FOR SUCCESS

The first thing you should do should be the easiest and the most motivating. Prepare yourself before you tackle the hard things. For instance, one of my wife's friends starts her morning by turning on a praise tape, closing her eyes, and worshiping the Lord for the first ten minutes. I read a spiritual biography or spiritual life book for a while—it gets my battery charged. The key is to start with whatever you find is the easiest, most enjoyable, and most immediately encouraging. There's also nothing more spiritual than to immediately start praying. But if I started with prayer, I'm afraid that half the time I would fall back asleep! Darlene Marie starts her morning with prayer and praise, then reads her Bible, then writes in her journal, and finally ends with additional prayer. The order is important but specific to you.

Second, when you are ready to turn your heart toward the Lord, stop and prepare yourself for Him. Close your eyes and quiet your heart. Bring all your thoughts into sharp focus on the throne room in the heavenlies. Bring every thought under control, and do not permit distracting thoughts to steal your attention. For the first few months, this may take more than a few moments, but don't become frustrated. Eventually, bringing your heart and mind into focus will take only a few seconds.

Third, follow your schedule point by point, in the same order, every day. Don't skip a step, no matter how much you're tempted. Discipline yourself and do not permit the "avoidance temptation" to conquer your resolve. This avoidance urge can be quite strong but must be absolutely conquered. Put your finger on the step you're working through in your devotions, and don't move on to the next step until you have finished that step. When this happens to me, I take careful note of it and put a little star in the margin to alert me to the spiritual opposition.

Whatever you do, don't permit your focus to leave the Lord and what you are committed to do. As you remain focused on Jesus Christ, the opposition will break down and depart. Don't doubt this principle. Just recently I unexpectedly experienced this very thing while addressing an item on my prayer list, and I remembered that such opposition had occurred in the days before when I prayed regarding this issue. Why? I don't know and don't necessarily need to know—I just upgraded my fervency and broke through. In the future I'm going to come to this step with commitment and dependence upon the Lord that the opposition will flee.

As you remain focused on Jesus Christ, the opposition will break down and depart.

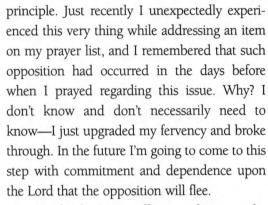

Fourth, don't ever allow anything to take the place of the two absolutes: prayer and the Word of God. Never allow any book, no matter how good, to take the place of reading His Word. Never allow yourself to skip or shorten the amount of time you pray before the Lord. Regardless of what else you do during your personal devotions, at least 50 percent of your total time should be focused on prayer and the Word.

Why not take a piece of paper and develop your first devotional schedule right now? Start revising it after you try it tomorrow morning. If it's your first year, don't try more than three or four things or you'll be exercising with too heavy of weights. Value the habit more than the difficulty or depth at this point. Put these basics in the order you think you would enjoy them best:

Bible reading
Prayer
Praise

Journaling

Reading a Christian book

What happens if you miss a day? Or a week? Even a month? Prepare yourself to restart this holiness habit and begin again! Don't try to catch up on your reading—just skip what you missed. Never construct a mountain you must conquer in order to "pay" for neglecting the Lord. Christ paid for all your sins and mine. His payment was sufficient for the Father, so it also must be for you. Just apologize to the Lord and receive His forgiveness and warm embrace.

MEDITATE ON SCRIPTURE

Of all the specific holiness habits, reading the Word of God is the absolute highest priority. Although you may think that prayer is the secret to transformation, I do not believe the Bible teaches that. Rather, the Bible is the *primary transforming agent*. Obviously, the Holy Spirit is the ultimate transformer, but He uses the Word of God as His primary tool.

Notice how the apostle Paul describes this transformation in Romans 12:2: "Be transformed by the renewing of your mind." Transformation begins with the believer's mind, not his behavior. As the Bible makes clear, all of us behave in accordance with what we believe. In fact, there is never an exception. When I have sinned, I somehow rationalize that sinning is in my best interest. Otherwise I wouldn't have sinned. So when I truly believe that the best option is obedience, I will choose obedience.

What I believe determines how I behave. Since that is true, the critical issue is for my mind to be changed to mirror what the Bible teaches. Usually, our minds are changed neither instantly nor in a sudden flash, but little by little as we believe more and more of the truth.

Paul identified transformation as a process with his choice of the word *renewing*, which literally means "to make new again." And again and again. The believer must make his mind new, over and over, until every thought from the "old" way of thinking has been rooted out and everything from the "new" (biblical) way of thinking has been firmly planted.

Transformation occurs by *renewing our minds* by the Bible, not merely by reading the Bible. Although reading the Bible certainly influences our lives in many wonderful ways, transformation only occurs as our minds are changed from believing a lie to believing the truth. If we don't allow the Bible to adjust the way we think, then the daily act of reading alone won't magically transform our behavior. Never forget these famous words of D. L. Moody: "The Bible wasn't given for our information, but our transformation." Read the Bible for transformation through the renewing of your mind.

Renew Your Mind by Annually Reading the Whole Bible or New Testament

The habit of reading through the Bible or New Testament every year is a wonderful practice that hundreds of thousands of committed believers follow each year. Nothing is better for general spiritual vitality than reading through large passages from the Bible day after day.

Renew Your Mind by Meditating on Carefully Selected Verses

Unlike reading through large sections of the Bible, this habit carefully selects small passages that focus specifically on those areas you know need to be transformed to fully please the Lord.

How do you know which verses to meditate on? Watch your behavior and monitor your attitudes, and whenever you find anything that isn't duplicating Jesus, that's your meditation agenda! Find three to five verses or sections in the Bible that deal directly with your problem area. Type or write out these verses on three-by-five cards and start reading them out loud every day. Dedicate at least one month to each area; you won't be able to renew your mind fully in only a few days. Meditate on these verses while asking the Lord to show you the lie that must be discarded and the truth that must take its place.

Each time you read these verses, put a mark on the bottom of each card and stay on target until you uncover the lie that was the power behind your sin. Then carefully and actively renew your mind until you know your mind has changed and you see reality differently.

Then, when the cluster of sins surrounding that particular lie is no longer part of your life, you can stop meditating on that specific topic—your transformation worked! The point of scriptural meditation isn't to meditate, but to be completely transformed in that particular area. The process is only valuable, therefore, to the extent to which it brings transformation.

So many well-meaning believers memorize Scripture without any transformation, thinking that if they can just remember the verses the transformation will automatically and supernaturally take place. Memorizing Scriptures puts them in your "memory banks" so you can meditate upon them—so you then can be transformed by them. If memorization is the goal, then memorization becomes an end in itself rather than the means of achieving a biblical transformation.

If you really want Scripture memory to transform your life, select an area of your life that needs transformation. Label that area with a word, such as *anger, stealing, lust,* or *gossip.* Then find the best three to five passages in the Bible that give clear statements of truth and directives about that problem, and write them down on a three-by-five card. Carry them with you everywhere and read them out loud over and over again. Think through every single word and seek the wisdom that lies in each verse.

Pray and ask the Lord to reveal the lies you believe in this area; then confess the sins you have committed, one at a time. Make sure to identify what you used to believe (the lie) but now know isn't biblical, and state the biblical truth with its godly attitudes and behaviors: "The Bible teaches that..." Depend actively upon the Holy Spirit to enable you in your commitment to know the truth and enjoy freedom in obedience to the Lord.

The point isn't how many verses you have memorized, but how many areas of your life have been transformed! You are not collecting verses as trophies. The only trophy that heaven celebrates is your life of holiness.

Renew Your Mind by Praying the Scriptures

This is a wonderful habit of holiness for you to practice on a regular basis. Take Scriptures that are particularly meaningful to you and pray them back to the Lord. Easy passages to do this with come from Psalms, Proverbs, Ephesians, Colossians, and Philippians. As you pray these Scriptures to the Lord, a different part of your life will be influenced and transformed. Usually, meditation touches your mind while prayerful meditation touches both your mind and your heart.

As you read and meditate on Scripture, record personal notes and insights right in your biblical text. Add dates when the Lord especially spoke to you through a particular passage. One of my earliest Bible professors showed us his Bible in class one day—it had lines and arrows and colors and circles and notes everywhere! I wondered if I should do that to my Bible. Now, over thirty years later, I would strongly encourage you to do that very thing. Whenever I reach over to pick up my Bible, I always simultaneously pick up that blue or red pen to mark right in the text what I learn.

The Bible is a priceless gift from the Lord for the entire body of Christ. The more you bring your life in line with the Bible, the more you will experience the fulfillment of God's promise of your transformation into the very image of Jesus Christ.

Chapter 11

The Habit of Journaling

Holiness appeared to me to be of a sweet, pleasant, charming,
serene, calm nature; which brought an inexpressible purity,
brightness, peacefulness, and ravishment to the soul.
In other words, that it made the soul like a field or garden of God,
with all manner of pleasant flowers.

JONATHAN EDWARDS

*F*irst you lie in your crib, then you lift your head, then you
rock back and forth, then you crawl, then you stand, then
you stagger, then you walk, then you trot, then finally you
run. First you count, then you add, then you subtract, then you
multiply, then you divide, then you work algebraic equations, then
you work in geometry, and finally you work in trigonometry.

In all areas of life, first steps are always followed by intermediate steps, followed by advanced steps. We have already discussed
the habits of daily devotions and biblical meditation. We will now
explore habits that build upon those earlier foundational habits of
holiness. Four additional advanced habits of holiness will be cov-
ered in the next chapter. If you will practice and eventually master

all six habits of holiness, I can promise that your life will experience a radical transformation into the wonderful image of Jesus Christ.

THE PRAYER JOURNAL

Of all the spiritual disciplines, I believe that prayer is more preached about but less practiced than any other. Many feel that prayer is at once the easiest and yet most difficult habit to develop.

If the Bible is the basic tool for renewing your mind, then prayer is the basic tool for renewing your relationship with the Lord. Prayer is the language of relationship and opens the portal of intimacy between the human and the divine. Without a vital prayer life, your walk of holiness will be only a one-sided attempt at human improvement. Prayer is the glue of relationship that connects your heart with the Lord's.

Prayer opens the portal of intimacy between the human and the divine.

Not only is prayer the language of relationship, but God designed prayer to be the primary tool to release supernatural answers to your wishes, hopes, and desires and to life's impossible or emergency situations. Although some people believe that God doesn't intervene supernaturally today, the Bible overflows with commands to seek that very thing—a supernatural answer. What is a supernatural answer? When God hears and answers your prayer, you are the recipient of a purposeful change in the natural that God supernaturally made happen just for you—and at the time you need it.

When you have seen the Lord answer your prayers time after time, your confidence in the power of prayer will become unshakeable and certain. In fact, the more you see the Lord answer you, the more you will be encouraged to pray for things you never would have dreamed of asking God to provide. The Bible is remarkably clear and completely consistent in what it says about prayer: "Most assuredly, I say to you, whatever you ask the Father in My name *He will give you.* Until now you have asked nothing in My name. Ask, and *you will receive,* that your joy may be full" (John 16:23–24).

Does the Lord have any requirements for answering your prayers?

"If you abide in Me, and My words abide in you, you will ask *what you desire,* and it shall be done for you." (John 15:7)

Notice that the first word is *if,* which usually precedes a condition to be fulfilled for the answer to be granted. "Abiding in Christ" is required (in John 15:7) for the fulfillment of such an incredible promise of answered prayer. But Christ also says, "My words abide in you." James 5:16–18 links the prayers of a righteous man to their answers: "The effective, fervent prayer of a righteous man avails much. Elijah was a man with a nature like ours, and he prayed earnestly that it would not rain; and it did not rain on the land for three years and six months. And he prayed again, and the heaven gave rain, and the earth produced its fruit."

This passage is remarkable because its main thesis is that a New Testament believer can experience supernatural answers to prayer, just as the Old Testament prophet Elijah did. His prayers literally stopped all normal rain for three years. Thus God gives answers to those who are righteous and pray "fervently."

Asking in His Name

There is no doubt as to why people are not seeing many answers to prayer these days: They are neither walking in intimate relationships with Christ nor walking in obedience to His Word. Therefore, they cannot inherit the magnificent but conditional promises of God giving them what they desire—and the incredible joy that such answers bring. Don't miss these remarkable and direct statements made about prayer by Jesus Himself:

> And whatever you ask in My name, that I will do, that the Father may be glorified in the Son. If you ask anything in My name, I will do it. (John 14:13–14)

> Ask what you desire, and it shall be done for you. (John 15:7)

> ...that whatever you ask the Father in My name He may give you. (John 15:16)

> Most assuredly, I say to you, whatever you ask the Father in My name He will give you. Until now you have asked nothing in My name. Ask, and you will receive, that your joy may be full. (John 16:23–24)

Do you know what many believers have done with these verses? Basically, cut them out of the New Testament. Why? Because Christians have decided they don't work, and if they don't work then they can't be true! Is that the truth? No. If the clear and repeated teachings of the Bible aren't working in our lives, it's not because the Bible has suddenly become untrue, *but rather because we have stopped fulfilling the requirements for those promises.*

Return to those passages and search out the conditions Jesus specifically attached to those promises. Fulfill those conditions, pray fervently in faith, and just watch the Lord keep His promises to you!

A few years ago, I was in a deep discussion about this very issue with a close friend who is a prayer warrior. I'll never forget what happened in the next twenty minutes or so. This prayer warrior simply smiled and brought out his prayer journal from his nearby desk drawer. It was April 30, 1998. He flipped back page after page in his prayer journal until January 1, 1996 and counted right before my eyes three hundred and sixty-eight different prayers the Lord answered in those two years and four months. God said yes to three hundred and sixty-eight of this man's specific prayers!

I sat dumbfounded.

Can you imagine having such a wonderful prayer life? He was beaming and at times laughed as he shared some of the more remarkable and miraculous answers to prayer he had experienced. Amazing! As he closed his prayer journal, I realized that the Lord's promises regarding prayer had been fulfilled in this man's life!

Why all this discussion about the fact that God actually still answers prayers—lots of them? Because the Lord commands you to pray to Him for answers so He can give them to you and cause your joy to overflow, as with my friend. The only problem? You must abide with Him and walk in holiness. Such a small price for such an overwhelming reward!

Keep my commandments…just as I have kept my Father's…that your joy may be full. (John 15:10–11)

Nearly everyone who advances beyond the most basic level of praying uses a prayer journal of one kind or another. Until I committed to becoming a man of prayer and established my own regular practice with a prayer journal, my prayer life produced more guilt than anything else!

The most practical prayer journal I have discovered is a medium-size three-ring binder with plastic tabs—buy a bunch of different colors of paper and make your own notebook. You'll get some ideas in the pages that follow, but here are three practical tips on maximizing your prayer life in your pursuit of holiness.

Standardize Your Prayer Schedule

By establishing a daily and weekly routine to follow when you pray, you destroy the three greatest hindrances to praying. The most common hindrance is not having a set place, time, and procedure to follow. When you schedule your focused prayer time, praying becomes very natural. For instance, I discovered that prayer works best for me *after* I have spent time journaling and reading God's Word, whereas Darlene Marie does exactly the opposite. Again, select the best order for you and, after some initial experimentation, don't change it.

The second most common hindrance to prayer is not knowing *what* to pray when you *want* to pray. Without establishing the *what* ahead of time, you will spend more time and energy trying to decide what to do than you will praying.

The third most common hindrance to praying is what I call the "wandering mind," which seems to plague nearly everyone in the early stages of learning to pray. By establishing a fixed track to pray, the opportunities for a wandering mind to derail you rapidly decrease and even disappear.

Listed below are some of the categories that you can select from to develop your own prayer schedule. Be careful, however, to start slowly and work in a limited number of categories in the beginning. Four to six prayer categories is plenty for the first year or so.

Sin

Confess all known sin and quietly wait on the Lord, making sure that your heart is clean before Him in all areas.

Self

Confess your independent nature; die to self; enthrone Christ. Humble yourself before Him, establishing Him as your Lord and Master. Present yourself to Him as a living sacrifice. Present the parts of your body as weapons for His usage this day.

Spiritual Strongholds

Confess all strongholds you are seeking to pull down, and experience renewal through Scripture meditation. Renew your mind in prayer by confessing all known unbiblical thoughts and actions. Ask the Lord to shower His mercy and grace upon you and work deeply in you.

Sanctification Prayers

These are requests you will pray for the rest of your life regarding your desire to become more like Christ in specific areas. These are never fully answered, for there is always more of Christ.

Spirit of God

Recommit not to grieve or quench the Holy Spirit. Ask the Holy Spirit to fill you for service this day. Depend upon Him for guidance, wisdom, strength, and leadership.

Spiritual Gifts

Thank the Lord for the gifts He has given you. Ask Him to deepen each of those gifts by name and cleanse you from any pride or selfish ambition you may have about His gifts in you. Petition the Lord to help you direct more of your energy toward using those gifts for His glory.

Spiritual Vision

Ask the Lord for His vision for your life, your marriage, your family, and the places you serve Him, including your church. Center your mind in the heavenlies, and seek to see your life from the Lord's perspective.

Spiritual Service

Pray for the specifics of the day, including all major responsibilities, meetings with individuals, important decisions, and so on.

Spiritual Warfare

Put on the whole armor of God, one piece at a time, making sure nothing is out of place. Recommit to stand and resist the enemy. Ask the Lord to keep you away from temptation, and commit to choosing obedience.

Spiritual Wisdom

Ask for the mind of Christ and His thoughts for the challenges of the day. Ask for financial stewardship and generosity. Ask for wisdom from above that is pure, peaceable, and willing to yield.

Spiritual Thanksgiving

Thank the Lord for at least ten new things you are thankful for. Don't leave this section until your heart is rejoicing with gratitude.

Spiritual Goals

Pray for each major goal for the year, asking for the Lord's wisdom, patience, grace, and empowerment.

Spiritual Intercession

Pray for each member of your family, extended family members, people with whom you work, church friends, people that don't know the Lord yet, your pastor and other Christian leaders, the president of the United States, and people you are mentoring.

Specific Prayers

These are requests that are concrete. You'll know for sure when these are answered with a yes, no, or not now.

Write Your Requests in Your Prayer Journal

Motivation in prayer is undoubtedly one of the doors that must be unlocked for an enduring and fulfilling life of prayer. When God created us, He linked the motivation we feel to the things that are truly important to us, and to the people we love. The more important something is to us, the more motivated we feel to move in that direction.

So, as I finish praying through specific requests from previous days, I now ask myself what I would like to see the Lord answer for me today. Then, as things come to my mind that are important to me and wouldn't be in disagreement with His will or His ways, I write those specific requests in my prayer journal. Then the next day, the prayer requests that are the newest on my list are truly the most timely and important. Since initiating this practice, motivation has never again been a problem in my prayer life!

As I pray through these specific requests, I see if the Lord has answered any of the requests since yesterday and then mark them off. What an exciting daily adventure!

Here's a format that seems to work really well:

NUMBER	SPECIFIC REQUEST	DATE STARTED	DATE ANSWERED	NUMBER OF DAYS	YES / NO
1					
2					
3					

Number: The number is the number of this request. For instance, if you started this today you might think of five important prayer requests and you would number them 1 through 5. Tomorrow, after you prayed through requests one through five, your next specific prayer request would be recorded as number 6.

Specific Request: On this one line write the specific request you want the Lord to answer. It has to be very specific so you will know if the Lord has answered it, but it doesn't necessarily need a completion date. I once put deadlines on my prayer requests merely because I didn't want to wait—and I learned that by doing that I was trying to put the Lord in a box, to make Him hurry up and answer my prayers according to my timetable.

Date Started/Date Answered: These are the dates on which you first write your prayer request in your prayer journal and when you know the Lord's answer.

Number of Days: I want to get a handle on how many days I prayed before the Lord answered my prayers. I counted the number of days between the date I started praying the request and the date the Lord answered the request and put the number off to the right of that specific request. Looking down a page of prayer requests where every request was answered, here's what that page looked like: 181 days, 148 days, 12 days, 90 days, 120 days, 2 days, 54 days, 60 days, 75 days, 15 days, 15 days, 60 days, 90 days, 164 days, 15 days.

Yes/No: When the answer comes from the Lord, I always write His answer in the form of a "Yes" or a "No" or "0" if something unusual comes up and the answer is no longer possible. I put these on the far right side of the line with a box around them. What an encouragement! So, as I turn the pages, I look down the far right column looking for an empty box and pray specifically for that request. But, as you can imagine, every page has a number of "yes" and "no" boxes, so the daily process alone tends to deeply encourage me to continue praying. Looking back over God's most recent answers for my prayers, here's what the yes/no box looks like: yes, yes, yes, no, no, yes, yes, yes, yes, yes, yes, yes, yes, yes, no.

This prayer habit deepens your consecration to Him. The miraculous answers to prayers that you record will utterly convince you that the Lord God is intimately involved in your life!

Set a Lifetime Prayer Goal

Every once in a while, the business world surfaces a concept that becomes very helpful to those of us in ministry. One of the better statistical concepts in recent years is something called benchmarking, a method of establishing the highest standard of excellence, which then becomes the new standard to measure one's performance against. At Walk Thru the Bible, of which I used to be president, the various ministries developed their own internal benchmarks. For instance, when the seminar ministry was in its twenty-third year, they identified the year in which they performed the best in several categories, including the following:

1. Total number of seminars in one year
2. Total number of seminar attendees in one year
3. Total number coming to know Christ in one year
4. Total number expressing a life-changing spiritual experience in one year
5. Total number committing to read the Bible regularly in one year

These standards then became practical measurements that the seminar team tried to improve on each year. For instance, in 1997 in the United States, Walk Thru the Bible established a new benchmark of sixteen hundred seminars in just twelve months. Two years later the vice president of seminars lifted that bar of excellence and sought to top two thousand seminars in just twelve months.

What measure are you using in your prayer life? I believe it is wise for a steward to have three specific measures to evaluate his life. First, use a biblical measure whenever you can find one. Second, use the standard of performance that you achieved for the Lord last year, and seek to improve it in both quality and quantity. Third, find the highest benchmark you can in that area and place that out in the far distance as the finish line you would love to reach before you meet the Lord at the end of your life.

I call the highest benchmark anyone has set in a particular area his or her "life benchmark." Obviously, Jesus Christ is the final life benchmark in many areas of my life, but in others, He wasn't called by the Father to achieve the same goals the Father assigned in my race. Remember, Jesus was able to say He finished the work that God assigned to Him, but He never was called to write a book!

I didn't have much difficulty figuring out who among us received more answers to prayer than anyone else. Although others have written classics on prayer, and others may have had more dramatic answers to prayer, I don't know of anyone who has even come close to the man who lived his life purposely to prove that God answers prayer: George Mueller. Before he died, he had recorded over ten thousand specific answers to prayer that God granted him during his lifetime.

Not long ago, Darlene Marie, Jessica, and I had the pleasure of skiing for a week in Colorado. We stayed at a close friend's mountain cabin. As we rode those ski lifts for thousands of feet, literally into the clouds, we felt like we were walking on the underside of heaven itself! I'll never forget one snowy afternoon breaking through the clouds into the brilliant sunshine and staring at a magnificent vision of the entire mountain range. It was breathtaking.

When I consider the mountain George Mueller scaled in prayer before the Lord, I can't help but call this prayer life benchmark anything less than "Mueller's Summit."

Why not join me in this exhilarating quest of following in the footsteps of this giant prayer warrior? Although I'm afraid I'm still in the far distant foothills, I'm committed to staying focused on the goal of George Mueller's ten thousand answered prayers and not looking back. Maybe someday before I meet the Lord, by God's grace I'll be able to break through those clouds and at least get a glimpse of that magnificent but distant "Mueller's Summit." So put on your hiking boots, bend your knee, and write out Prayer Request #1.

YOUR LIFE JOURNAL

My wife loves to write letters, but I don't. In fact, over my lifetime I have started at least six or seven journals and then thrown them in the bottom dresser drawer, out of sight and mind, within three weeks of starting each one! And if I'm not mistaken, every single one of those false starts began with the date January 1 and probably had the last record somewhere between February and March.

Ever started, restarted, and restarted again? And then finally given up? When it came to writing a journal, I found it was considerably beyond my greatest intentions. And as you might expect if you've been tracking with me through this book, the life journal didn't work for me earlier because of the lack of other underlying spiritual disciplines that *also* didn't exist. I was trying to build the "fifth-floor spiritual discipline" without floors three and four!

But something happened when I was thirty-eight that changed all that. In the middle of a rather difficult midlife crisis, I flew across the country to see a man who specialized in the development and growth of Christian leaders. After discussing with me on the phone my desire to quit the ministry and hearing my frustration and despair, he invited me to fly out and spend the afternoon with him.

What he shared with me that day marked my life forever. The first thing he asked was for me to share my life story. When I had reviewed it up to approximately two years prior to the present, he stopped me and asked if he could finish the story. I quizzed him on how he could do that, but he only smiled and waited for me to listen. As he began to speak, I couldn't believe his insights! The longer he spoke, the greater was my amazement as he expressed exactly what had been happening to me.

After he finished, I asked if there was any help for such a person as me! He laughed and said, "You are right on schedule." Although I had no idea what that meant, I was deeply encouraged that perhaps things could turn out for good after all.

Then he put his hands in front of me with his left higher than his right. He said that early in my Christian life, my inner walk with the Lord was strong (the left hand) and my competence in ministry for the Lord was weak (the lower right hand). I nodded in agreement. Then he shared that in time, through Bible college and then seminary, my competence grew quickly but my walk with the Lord probably suffered. As he described that, he slowly elevated his right hand, representing competence, over his left hand, representing my inner walk of devotional holiness. I nodded in agreement and began to sense growing conviction.

Then he said the reason I was so tempted to leave the ministry was because my sense of fulfillment had been taken away by the Lord, and regardless of how hard I pushed myself into His work, it couldn't bring the fulfillment and joy that it did earlier—the Lord wouldn't permit it. I can remember wondering how he knew that.

He said, "The Lord knows that unless the positions of these two hands switch one more time, back to the original order, you will never become the spiritual leader God created you to be." Then he asked some very probing questions about the spiritual disciplines of my life. Although I practiced daily devotions, they often were shallow. Though I read my Bible regularly, recently I didn't receive much help or food from it. And, although I prayed, I certainly didn't pray as long as I wished or receive many answers to my prayers.

Once again, he smiled and nodded—with no condemnation in his voice or eyes. How I thank the Lord for him and his insight at that crisis point in my life! Then his lower hand, representing my walk with the Lord, began pushing against the competence hand. He said the Lord was deliberately and forcibly bringing pressure on me by taking away any fulfillment from *doing,* so I could embrace the deeper fulfillment of *being* once again.

He said there is a moment of conviction that the Lord brings in everyone's life when He calls them to walk *with* Him more than to work *for* Him and that the switch must come for me as well. Then this wise mentor shared that I must go back home and focus my best efforts on learning and practicing these spiritual disciplines.

And did he ever nail me on this life journal idea! He said the daily journal is an incredibly powerful tool to assist in the pilgrimage from doing to being.

That man was absolutely right. I dedicated myself to the Lord during those life-changing months and have never looked back. How I praise the Lord that those "hands" switched back to correct priorities. Now walking with the Lord is the high point of my life, not working for Him. Now my ministry is birthed in being, not in doing.

Tips for Life Journaling

Obviously, a whole book could easily be written on each of these spiritual disciplines, including how to experience great victory through maintaining a life journal. Here are a few of the secrets I have discovered:

1. Write in your life journal every day you have devotions.
2. Devote a whole page to each day.
3. Put your pen at the top of the page and don't take it off until the whole page is filled.
4. Give yourself about three months to get into the swing of it; don't be frustrated.
5. Release yourself to be completely honest, even with respect to sin.
6. Try as many different things as you can in your journal, and continue whatever helps you the most.

What should you write in your journal? Here's a list of some of the categories I use in mine. But please remember that, next year, I might have different ones. Use whatever works for you during this time in your life. If it isn't working, remain patient and continue trying while asking the Lord for wisdom. Keep at it! You might find it helpful to write about:

- your prayers to the Lord
- your insights from meditating on the Bible
- your confessions of sin (many people lock their journals)
- your frustrations and fears
- your private dreams and visions and desires
- your lessons from successes and failures
- your praise and worship to the Lord

There are some helpful Christian books on journaling that any good Christian bookstore could direct you to. Whatever format you choose, learn how to write to the Lord from your heart. If you read my journal, you would soon know me from the inside out—just the way the Lord knows me. The men and women who have begun this holiness habit have become wonderfully addicted to the joy of the journal!

Chapter 12

Praise and Fasting

*A holy life is a voice; it speaks when the tongue is silent,
and is either a constant attraction or a perpetual reproof.*

Robert Leighton

If you were to visit your local Christian bookstore and ask to be directed to books on the spiritual life or spiritual disciplines, you would no doubt find many outstanding books covering more than twenty different disciplines of the spiritual life. We will discuss only six of the disciplines in this book; but I have found that these six habits of holiness are vital to the spiritual walk of those believers who walk closely with the Lord and touch the world with their lives.

PRAISE AND WORSHIP

It's amazing. During what we call a worship service, nearly everything takes place during that hour *except* genuine worship. Worship is defined as the reverent act of offering extravagant respect, admiration, or devotion to the highest object of esteem, our Lord. *Worship* is derived from the concept of worthiness, or worth—to worship the Lord means we express to Him how we feel about His worth. Praise and worship are nothing more and nothing less than expressing to the Lord God, privately and publicly, what we think of His worthiness.

I was away from home, speaking at a weeklong leadership conference; so when Sunday morning rolled around, I attended a local worship service. During a less-than-stirring rendition of a grand hymn, I looked around at the people in my row and saw that fewer than a third were singing. And none of those who *were* singing seemed even remotely connected to the Lord at a moment meant to ascribe to our Creator value and worth.

Even as I write this, memories flood my heart of a very different experience months earlier. I had the privilege of speaking to a church in Singapore and, a week later, a church in Malaysia. At both services, the pastors opened by leading the congregation in a one-hour praise session—and no one sat down during the entire hour! Intense worship flooded the faces and echoed with the voices of thousands. How the Lord must have relished the adoration of His people!

Back in America, two recent movements have brought to the church a renewed emphasis on praise and worship. The first is the charismatic movement; the second is Promise Keepers (PK). I've spoken at numerous PK stadium events, and I've seen it happen many times—men who have never truly worshiped the Lord at any time in their lives become initiated into the wonders of praise and worship. At first they sing hymns like they always do. Then they begin to sing from their hearts and grasp the meaning of the words.

Then they begin to connect with the Lord while they are singing. Finally they become enraptured with the Lord and cannot stop praising Him. Once men have tasted the fruit of true biblical praise, they never want to go back to praiseless praise services and worshipless worship services.

But the tragedy is that they do. In fact, many men and women never learn how to praise and worship on their own without the support of a praise gathering, worship conference, or PK event.

As far as we know, the Lord bestowed the gifts of praise and worship on only two groups among His immense number of created beings: angels and mankind. Just because the Lord created our innate ability and desire to worship, however, doesn't mean that we use it for the purpose for which He gave it.

Unless we make full use of this incredible gift of praise, believers will remain limited in their growth and will experience life only on the earthly plane. Millions of Christians "go to worship" year after year and never truly connect with the Lord on a deeply personal, radically transforming level.

Expressing His Worthiness

A believer can do daily devotions and never praise and worship. A believer can attend church weekly and never praise and worship. A believer can pray regularly and never praise and worship. So do *you* praise and worship the Lord? If so, are you a "worship codependent"? Do you only praise Him in a group environment at a set time and place?

When then does true praise and worship take place? When a person really connects with the Lord in order to express how wonderful He is. Worship is an intimate interaction in which a believer "compliments" the Lord so personally and directly that he feels he is the only person in the Lord's presence at the time.

I'm convinced that so few believers truly worship the Lord because they are out of touch with His greatness and power. When we enter into the Lord's presence at death, we will immediately and intensely worship and praise the Lord. Worship is the immediate and innate response to the presence and power of God. Individuals who know the Lord and His glory are always ready to worship. Individuals who don't worship are often blinded by their own glory.

If you do not truly worship the Lord, you are out of touch with His greatness and power

That's why worship is the fifth habit of holiness discussed here instead of the first, second, or third—believers frequently don't worship on an ongoing and meaningful basis unless the other disciplines are in place. Unless they are engaged in regular devotions, biblical meditation, and prayer, believers tend to be so focused on themselves that they can never break through to experience the true majesty of God.

This is also true in a group dynamic. Unless a worship leader knows how to direct the people to truly praise the Lord in worship, an organized service can actually *hinder* worship. Too often the congregation's focus is on the singing of a song rather than worshiping the Person to whom the song is being sung. Our focus has to move away from the process so that our singing can carry and deliver the heart's praise. We must somehow make the transition from the act of singing to the act of praising. The words and the pace of the singing must become secondary so that we can reach out with our hearts to express unbridled praise and adoration for our loving Father.

Learning a new praise song each week can become a hindrance to praising the Lord, until the congregation knows the songs well enough to sing it to the Lord rather than focusing on the words and melody. Many of the newer songs have a simple melody and often very simple words. Some have criticized modern praise songs as lacking depth, but many believe the primary purpose of singing is to worship the Lord, not to communicate deep doctrines.

The old hymns can be tremendous teaching tools; but remember, if the heart of the believer does not connect with the Lord in order to express His worthiness, then biblical praise and worship do not occur regardless of how good the music is. The Lord doesn't want to be serenaded; He wants to be worshiped.

The part of the Sunday morning service in which the pastor preaches is sometimes labeled in the bulletin as "worship through preaching." Once again, worship may or may not occur through the preaching. I know that when I hear some men of God in the pulpits, they lift up the Lord so effectively that I cannot help myself—I must thank and praise the Lord! The higher the pastor lifts up the Lord, the more I spontaneously worship the Lord from my heart.

Unfortunately, in other pulpits—even those with solid, Bible-teaching preachers—the Lord isn't lifted up so that the audience is moved to worship Him alone. Sermon after sermon opens the meaning of the biblical text, but rarely does the pastor fulfill his greatest calling—to lead the heart of the congregation into the glorious presence of the Lord, where they are overwhelmed by His grace and glory and respond to Him in sincere worship, praise, and obedience.

Sermons must move in stages from focusing on the pastor, to focusing on the need of the audience, to focusing on the Bible, to ultimately focusing on the Lord Himself. If the final "amen" is spoken before the needy hearts of His people touch the heart of their God, then unfortunately a tragic abortion has occurred in the preaching process.

But now, let me shift the focus from the music and preaching back to you.

Personal Worship

Our most meaningful worship should occur *between* Sundays, not *on* Sundays. Sunday is a time to come together to praise and worship corporately, but it shouldn't be the only time you praise and worship the Lord. Why not? Because the Lord's greatness doesn't decrease when you walk out of the church service, so your response to Him shouldn't change!

Of course, this is not a book on worship, but on holiness. The habit of praise produces holiness in two directions. First, when you set yourself apart to ascribe glory and strength to the Lord, you dedicate yourself to that sacred purpose. Second, when you lift up the Lord and set Him apart and above everything and everyone else, you make Him holy in your heart. The more you lift the Lord up in your mind and set Him apart in His magnificence, the more you worship Him in the beauty of holiness. The more your heart praises His holiness, the more you will begin to live more deeply in that holiness.

Throughout this book, I have fought the natural desire to write about the Lord's holiness rather than ours. This book is focused specifically upon *our* holiness, especially during times of temptation. But perhaps a slight glimpse into His holiness may be permissible.

When you cross the final threshold and enter the presence of the Lord, you will find the twenty-four elders, the four living creatures, the host of angels, and millions of believers all singing of the Lord! Here is how the apostle John describes what they will be singing:

> "You are worthy to take the scroll, and to open its seals; for You were slain, and have redeemed us to God by Your blood out of every tribe and tongue and people and nation, and have made us kings and priests to our God; and we shall reign on the earth...."
>
> And I heard the voice of many angels around the throne, the living creatures, and the elders; and the number of them was ten thousand times ten thousand, and thousands of thousands, saying with a loud voice: "Worthy is the Lamb who was slain to receive power and riches and wisdom, and strength and honor and glory and blessing!" (Revelation 5:9–12)

John's vision climaxes with this revelation. Don't miss who says this.

> And every creature which is in heaven and on the earth and under the earth and such as are in the sea, and all that are in them, I heard saying: "Blessing and honor and glory and power be to Him who sits on the throne, and to the Lamb, forever and ever!" (v. 13)

When we see the Lord and know the truth about Him and what He has done and is doing and will do, we will not be able to stop our hearts from bursting with inexpressible and inexhaustible praise and worship.

And what will we sing? "You are worthy!"

When you believe the truth about the true worthiness of the Lord, you will not be able to stop yourself from worshiping Him. And when you want to express your heart, filled with wonder and gratitude and adoration, you want just one person to hear it—the Lord. When you care enough to reach out and express to Him that He is worthy, you will have entered through the portal of praise.

Fervent with the Lord

Another key trait of biblical praise is that you connect with the Lord *fervently*. The Bible gives remarkably diverse instructions about how we should praise and worship our God. The guidelines aren't hidden in complicated passages, and you don't need to learn Greek or Hebrew to understand them. In fact, they are spelled out as clearly as any other major teaching of the Bible.

So what's the problem? Many of our denominations and churches have selected and followed a few Bible passages on praise and worship while summarily excluding and avoiding the rest of the passages, which are just as direct and biblical as the ones they have chosen to affirm and practice. And too often they attack the practices of the other groups whose approved practices of praise and worship are different.

As I traveled around the world and ministered among many different denominations and groups, my eyes were forced open to my own narrow-mindedness! I can remember actually sweating in some services because I didn't know what to do with my hands. In other nations I worried because I didn't know what to do with my feet. I remember other situations in which I bit my lip because I didn't know what to say out loud when others were shouting.

You see, I was raised in a great church in a wonderful tradition. But looking back now, I realize we practiced from a passive position of praise. The less, the better. The quieter, the more biblical. The darker the clothes, the holier. The slower the tempo, the deeper the praise. But I couldn't find instructions for this type of worship in Scripture. Finally, I realized that I must find out exactly what the Lord instructed His people to do in praise and worship.

What I found was that God instructs us to worship Him *fervently.* How fervent are you in your praise and worship? Think through the past week and rate yourself on a scale from one to a hundred on the fervency of your praise and worship.

How fervent are you when cheering your favorite singer at a concert?

How about when you're rooting for your favorite football team?

How fervent were you the last time you read the Psalms?

If your praise and worship languish around the thirty mark, not only will the Lord not be too impressed, but neither will you return very often to the corridors of praise.

Psalm 150 captures this attitude of fervent praise and worship—I call it the "Hallelujah Chorus of the Old Testament":

Praise the LORD!
> Praise God in His sanctuary;
Praise Him in His mighty firmament!
> Praise Him for His mighty acts;

Praise Him according to His excellent greatness!
Praise Him with the sound of the trumpet;
Praise Him with the lute and harp!
Praise Him with the timbrel and dance;
Praise Him with stringed instruments and flutes!
Praise Him with loud cymbals;
Praise Him with clashing cymbals!
Let everything that has breath praise the Lord.
Praise the Lord!

Notice the exclamation points and specific instructions. When a person becomes fervent, his or her voice is often raised and the body becomes more animated. For a quick study on what fervency looks like, just watch a college football or basketball game and listen to the people in the stands. Watch what they do, especially when the score is close and the game is nearing the end. No one will be seated; no one will be quiet; and no one will have his hands in his pockets. Why? Because fervency must demonstrate itself *physically.*

Why should a religious service be any different? When a believer is fervent in praising and worshiping the Lord, it is difficult, if not impossible, to remain seated. The Bible doesn't command a certain posture for praise all of the time, and there's nothing inherently better about bowing your head to pray or lifting your head to pray. But you'll notice that the more intense the prayer or praise, the more people will begin to face heaven. When Christ prayed right before the famous feeding of the five thousand, this was his posture in prayer: "And He took the five loaves and the two fish, *and looking up to heaven,* He blessed and broke and gave the loaves to the disciples" (Matthew 14:19).

I've discovered this is also true of our hands. The more intense the worship, the more our hands find a reason to move upward. I've observed this phenomenon time and again at Promise Keepers conferences. On the opening Friday night, only a few scattered men are raising their hands during worship, and they probably feel a little out of place. On Saturday morning, about 30 to 40 percent lift their hands spontaneously when we sing "Amazing Grace." By the middle of the afternoon, when we are singing "Holy, Holy, Holy," you would be hard-pressed to find a man whose hands and face are not reaching toward the heart of heaven.

One's posture can also be linked to one's fervency. Searching through Scripture, I can't find the command "Sit and pray!" or "Sit and praise!" But I *can* find passages that tell us to stand or to kneel. Falling on your face is biblical; dancing is, too. So when you want to follow the biblical model, don't spend so much time *sitting* during prayer or praise. Some of the greatest men and women of God read the Bible only on their knees!

Will you join King David as he dances before the Lord with all his might?

Therefore ask yourself, *How do I feel about widening my comfort zone to the biblical norm in praise and prayer before the Lord?* Can you shout? Can you kneel? Would you lay prostrate? Do you ever weep in worship? Can you clap loudly and really get into it? Could you ever dance before the Lord in your living room (or basement) or in the forest? Will you join King David as he dances before the Lord with all his might? Or will you obey the psalms when they instruct you to praise with instruments?

Wrapped up in this freewheeling discussion about the style of your praise is an encouragement to loosen up a bit! Do you think when you get to heaven that heaven's choir will never clap their hands, stamp their feet, raise their voices, or shout "Glory!"? If heaven liberates us to express our praise more than a quiet and reserved "Amen" once every few years, perhaps we had better start practicing for the real thing!

The Lord Is Worthy

How many different reasons do you have to praise and worship the Lord? The more reasons you have to praise, the more potential you have to praise Him. If you can think of only five or six things to praise the Lord for, you'll soon run out of honest and meaningful praise and worship. Consider some of the many reasons you can praise the Lord.

The creation of the Lord is an incredible and almost infinite cause for praise. Everywhere you look, from your backyard to the far reaches of space, you can see the handiwork of the Master Creator. The more you know about any living organism, the more amazed and thankful you will be for His handiwork!

The compassions of the Lord are threaded throughout human history and throughout your own past, present, and future. An awareness of the Lord's compassion should provide you with a new list of things to praise Him for every day. Jeremiah speaks to this issue in Lamentations 3:22–23:

> Through the LORD's mercies we are not consumed, because His compassions fail not. They are new every morning; great is Your faithfulness.

Do you see the flow of the author's innate thought? Jeremiah saw a new reality of God's compassions and mercies that immediately turned his thoughts directly to the Lord. Great is His faithfulness!

The character of the Lord will become your most treasured focus of praise and worship the longer you walk with Him in habits of holiness. Why? Because the most precious thing about a friend is not what he does or says but who he is.

During the past decade of focused worship, I have noticed the Lord's character becoming more prominent in my praises than His promises, works, and prophecies. How I love to extol His tenderness, loyalty, compassion, patience, strength, wisdom, long-suffering, mercy, goodness, and kindness!

Here's what King David revealed about this incredible source of joy and pleasures that never end: "In Your presence is fullness of joy; at Your right hand are pleasures forevermore" (Psalm 16:11).

May each of us experience this fullness of joy through our worship of the Lord on this side of the eternal veil and enjoy right now the foretaste of pleasures forevermore!

FASTING

As you look across any shopping mall, visit any restaurant, or walk through the low-fat and diet aisles of a supermarket, you can quickly surmise that we are not a generation who believes in and practices fasting on a regular basis. Unfortunately, even most believers today are missing out on the benefits of this important spiritual discipline. But survey the Scriptures and you will find among those who fasted Moses, Samuel, David, Elijah, the Ninevites, Nehemiah,

King Darius, Daniel, Anna, Jesus, John the Baptist, the Pharisees, the apostles, Paul, and the early Christians.

What exactly is a biblical fast? Fasting is the voluntary denial of something for a specific time, for a spiritual reason, by an individual, couple, family, church, city, or nation. Does fasting work? In the Lord's sovereignty, He decided that whenever a person denies himself of food or sleep or speaking (silence) or the presence of others (solitude) for spiritual purposes, the spiritual consequences will be multiplied.

Remember, for instance, the difficulty the disciples were experiencing in Matthew 17:14–21 when they tried to heal a demon-possessed epileptic. Jesus explained to them, "This kind does not go out except by prayer and fasting." Normal prayer and procedures for demonic problems weren't powerful enough to expel this particular kind of demon. However, the Lord multiplies the power of prayer when His people fast and pray.

Believers sometimes choose to fast when battling in an area of their lives or addressing an issue that is of particular concern to them. Most people who fast don't do it because they enjoy it, but because it aids them in some way. Some fast to break free from a stubborn sin, to thank the Lord for a major answer to prayer, or to focus all their attention upon their relationship with the Lord.

You can fast to receive the Lord's guidance in an important decision, to repent and humble yourself before the Lord, or to seek the Lord's protection from war, tragedy, or destruction. Some believers fast to beseech the Lord to send revival.

But you aren't likely to fast unless you really need the answer to your prayers and know that the Lord is the only one who can meet your need. You won't fast unless you believe the Lord is powerful enough and interested enough in you to answer your prayers and intervene in the situation you face. You won't fast unless you have come to the conclusion that by denying yourself and humbling yourself before the Lord, your prayers will have a greater influence with Him.

How often should you fast? As often as you like. But whatever you do, don't stand up in a prayer meeting and ask for prayer as you endure your fast! As Jesus instructed, put on your best clothes and happiest face and veil your fasting from the eyes of men. What should you do when you are out to lunch or dinner with someone? Share that you aren't eating for "personal reasons" but you would love to enjoy their company.

Some people participate in an annual fast, selecting the same period of time each year to establish this holy habit in their lives. Others have made a habit of a weekly fast, fasting for the same twenty-four-hour period each week. A practical way to start is by fasting through the Sunday evening meal and Monday's breakfast and lunch, then eating again on Monday evening.

The Lord multiplies the power of prayer when His people fast and pray.

Try a quick fast when something really important arises and you are intently seeking the Lord's help. Purposefully skip one meal and get away by yourself for that time to focus solely on the Lord. A personal crisis will often thrust people into urgent fasts. If a terrible car accident put someone they loved into a life-threatening situation, many would stop eating just to continue praying for the Lord's intervention.

Some believers practice an occasional Daniel fast, eating

nothing but fruits and vegetables for a week. They partake of no coffee, soft drinks, bread, or dessert for fourteen days. Darlene Marie and I have found that the Daniel fast has nearly always resulted in a tremendous breakthrough on the sixth day—and we don't want to stop because of what the Lord is doing in our lives! The Daniel fast works well within a family context and permits you to deal with social responsibilities a bit more easily.

One spiritually mature pastor has been practicing a forty-day total fast every year for fourteen years. A large portion of his church joins him on this spiritual fast each year, and the number is growing. You should hear the stories of miraculous breakthroughs in the lives of individuals and the church as a whole.

Fasting is an advanced holiness habit but repays those who practice it with rich rewards in their walk with the Lord and holiness of life. If you aren't practicing any fasts in your life, why not try a Daniel fast for a week or longer? I can promise you from personal experience that you'll be thrilled you did!

LIVING A LIFE OF HOLINESS

May I complete this book by speaking to you personally? How are you doing with these holiness habits? Take a moment for a bit of reflection. Regardless of where you are in your pursuit of holiness right at this moment, don't be discouraged! The main issue isn't where you are today as much as where you will be tomorrow, this time next year, and in ten years. Take a broader look at life and realize you are called to be a steward of your life, and you are challenged by the Lord to progress in holiness and Christlikeness.

Of the holiness habits we have looked at, which one do you feel would make the most difference in your life if you were further down the road of mastery? That's the one you should start with first. Don't try to implement everything all at once because it is a guaranteed way to failure. Take the one you desire most and spend the next thirty days specifically focusing on it. It takes at least one to three months to build a solid spiritual habit.

Fight the natural tendency to want to fix everything today. Deny this temptation as it nearly always is from your fleshly pride seeking immediate perfection. Instead, enjoy victory and lasting life-change by succeeding in building one habit at a time. Just think what your life will be like in a couple of years!

Finally, let me offer a few parting words of encouragement.

Live under grace not under law. Don't become a legalistic slave to your holiness habits. Give yourself breathing room and don't be afraid to take a day or two off now and then. On Sunday, I have an entirely different routine; but by Monday morning, I'm more than ready to get back at it. You haven't committed a major sin by missing a day or even a few days—leave a little bit of room for the unexpected bumps that life brings us. The Lord more than understands!

Enjoy yourself more by adding variety to your schedule. If you are experiencing a bit of boredom or find it's getting harder to get up in the morning, then try this: Share with the Lord that you are going to sleep in tomorrow morning because you think you'll be better company after a little extra rest. Go to bed as early as you can and sleep in as late as you can. It's amazing what a few extra hours of sleep can do for a tired warrior! Then to recharge your batteries, find a really motivating Christian book or tape and fit it into your devotional schedule. I started doing this years ago, and by changing my reading diet regularly, interest and motivation hasn't been a problem.

Anticipate the joy of established holiness habits. After practicing these habits of holiness for a while, the benefits you receive will be so large and so meaningful, you won't want to miss them! Gone will be the days of having to muster all the self-discipline you can find to get up early and meet the Lord. Instead, you will find yourself waking with anticipation!

Holiness is a concept that can seem so big and so overwhelming that many have simply placed it in a personal procrastination box and hid it in their closets. I have found that if a person is to make progress in any problem area of life, two things must be true. First, the problem area must be made simple enough that he easily understands it and can explain it to someone else after hearing it once. Second, the path must be made clear enough that he instinctively knows the way. I hope I have accomplished both objectives for you in this book.

I want you to understand the big picture of holiness so well that you could explain it to a child. I hope that the path is now clear to you. And I pray that this book has been an encouragement to you in your personal pilgrimage toward holiness in these times of temptation.

I hold fast to your statutes, O LORD;
> do not let me be put to shame.
I run in the path of your commands,
> for you have set my heart free.
(Psalm 119:31–32, NIV)

World-Renowned Teacher Leads the Way to a Renewed Life

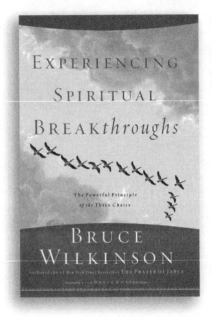

EXPERIENCING SPIRITUAL BREAKTHROUGHS

Craving "more" in your spiritual life? Join Bruce Wilkinson, author of the #1 *New York Times* bestseller *The Prayer of Jabez*, and blast through your spiritual logjam to find joy, peace, and a revitalized relationship with the Lord!

ISBN 1-57673-929-5

30 DAYS TO EXPERIENCING SPIRITUAL BREAKTHROUGHS

This thirty-day tool for spiritual growth presents thirty practical articles that show readers how to experience breakthroughs in their Christian lives, marriages, families, and walks with God.

ISBN 1-57673-982-1

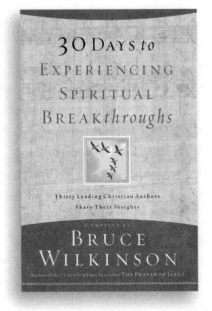

The BreakThrough Series, Book On[e]
The Prayer of Jabez

ISBN 1-57673-733-0

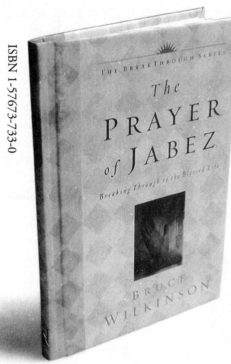

- #1 *New York Times* bestseller
- 11 million in print!
- www.prayerofjabez.com
- Book of the Year 2001 & 200[2]

"Fastest-selling book of all time[.]
—*Publishers Week[ly]*

- The Prayer of Jabez Audiocassette — ISBN 1-57673-842-6
- The Prayer of Jabez Audio CD — ISBN 1-57673-907-4
- The Prayer of Jabez for Women — ISBN 1-57673-962-7
- The Prayer of Jabez for Women Audiocassette — ISBN 1-57673-963-5
- The Prayer of Jabez Leather Edition — ISBN 1-57673-857-4
- The Prayer of Jabez Journal — ISBN 1-57673-860-4
- The Prayer of Jabez Devotional — ISBN 1-57673-844-2
- The Prayer of Jabez Bible Study — ISBN 1-57673-979-1
- The Prayer of Jabez Bible Study: Leader's Edition — ISBN 1-57673-980-5
- The Prayer of Jabez for Teens — ISBN 1-57673-815-9
- The Prayer of Jabez for Teens Audio CD — ISBN 1-57673-904-X
- The Prayer of Jabez Gift Edition — ISBN 1-57673-810-8

The BreakThrough Series, Book Two
Secrets of the Vine™

ISBN 1-57673-975-9

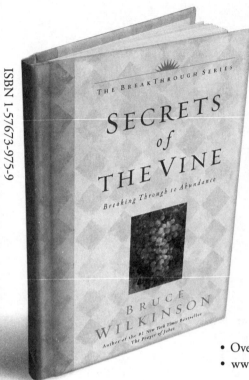

#2 *New York Times* Bestseller

- Over 3 million in print!
- www.thebreakthroughseries.com

The BreakThrough Series, Book Three
A Life God Rewards™

#1 New York Times Bestseller

www.thebreakthroughseries.com

- **A Life God Rewards Audio** ISBN 1-57673-978-3
- **A Life God Rewards Audio CD** ISBN 1-59052-007-6
- **A Life God Rewards Leather Edition** ISBN 1-59052-008-4
- **A Life God Rewards Journal** ISBN 1-59052-010-6
- **A Life God Rewards Devotional** ISBN 1-59052-009-2
- **A Life God Rewards Bible Study** ISBN 1-59052-011-4
- **A Life God Rewards Bible Study: Leader's Edition**

    ISBN 1-59052-012-2
- **A Life God Rewards Gift Edition** ISBN 1-59052-949-X

Also available from Multnomah Kidz:

- **A Life God Rewards for Kids** ISBN 1-59052-095-5
- **A Life God Rewards for Little Ones** ISBN 1-59052-094-7
- **A Life God Rewards, Girls Only** ISBN 1-59052-097-1
- **A Life God Rewards, Girls 90-Day Challenge**

    ISBN 1-59052-099-8
- **A Life God Rewards, Guys Only** ISBN 1-59052-096-3
- **A Life God Rewards, Guys 90-Day Challenge**

    ISBN 1-59052-098-X